Eco-Economics

Navigating the Path to a Sustainable Future

By
Sowmy VJ

Dedicated to my wife, Nithya, my son, Rohit, and all the wonderful professionals who have engaged with me in this research compilation, since 2018.

Table of Contents

Foreword: Setting the Stage for Sustainable Transformation 1

Introduction: The Concept of Eco-Economics 6

Preface: Understanding Eco-Economics 10

Chapter 1: Historical Context and Evolution 14

Chapter 2: The Business Case for Sustainability 18
    Profitability and Competitiveness 20
    Case Studies of Successful Companies 23

Chapter 3: The Financial Landscape of Sustainability 28
    Sustainable Investing: An Overview 29
    Key Financial Instruments and Mechanisms 32

Chapter 4: Embedding Sustainability in Corporate Strategy 38
    Steps to Integrate Sustainability 40
    Role of Leadership and Governance 44

Chapter 5: Metrics and Measurement 48
    Defining Key Performance Indicators (KPIs) 49
    Reporting Standards and Frameworks 51

Chapter 6: Driving Innovation Through Sustainability 54
    Green Technology and Innovation 55
    R&D for Sustainable Solutions 57

Chapter 7: Risk Management in a Sustainable Context 60
    Identifying and Mitigating Risks 62
    Building Resilience in Business Operations 65

Chapter 8: The Role of Policy and Regulation 69
Understanding Relevant Regulations 70
Engaging with Policymakers 72

Chapter 9: Stakeholder Engagement and Communication 75
Identifying Key Stakeholders 76
Effective Communication Strategies 79

Chapter 10: Financing the Sustainable Transformation 83
Accessing Capital for Sustainability Projects 84
Role of Banks and Financial Institutions 87

Chapter 11: The Impact on Human Capital 91
Retaining and Developing Quality Jobs 92
Training and Education for the Green Economy 95

Chapter 12: Community Investment and Social Impact 99
Corporate Social Responsibility (CSR) 100
Case Studies of Community Investment 103

Chapter 13: Global Trends and Future Outlook 108
Emerging Markets and Global Movement 109
Predicting Future Trends 112

Chapter 14: Overcoming Barriers to Sustainable Transformation ... 116
Common Challenges and Solutions 117
Stories of Overcoming Obstacles 120

Chapter 15: Taking Action: Your Role in Sustainable Transformation
.... 124
Personal Reflection and Commitment 125
Practical Steps for Immediate Action 127

Conclusion: A Roadmap to a Sustainable Future 130

Appendix A: Resources for Sustainable Business 133
Tools and Templates for Implementation 135

Foreword:
Setting the Stage for Sustainable Transformation

In the frozen stillness of dawn, there lies the potential for monumental change. We find ourselves at the cusp of a revolution, one that demands our collective will to reshape our world. This book emerges as a beacon for those who are daring enough to seek sustainable transformation in their business endeavours. Whether you're a seasoned professional at the height of your career or someone stepping into the realm of finance and investing, this text aims to ignite a passion for ecological and economic harmony.

Our journey begins here, in this foreword. This isn't just a preamble; it's the setting of a grand stage where the stakes are high, and the rewards even higher. Imagine standing at a crossroads where each path leads to a different future. One that embraces sustainability ushers us into a realm of enduring profitability and planetary wellbeing, while the other careens into uncharted and perilous territories.

I am Sowmy VJ, your navigational guide who will give you turn-by-turn instructions, but wouldn't annoy you with my opinion on your life. I am an asset manager, with 31 years of financial industry experience, based in London, and I run a firm, Helix.Earth which develops strategies and portfolios that track sustainable transformation in businesses that support our everyday lives. Enough of me, this is all about you. So, fasten your seat belt, and get set for the journey.

The world is changing at an unprecedented pace. In the wake of environmental turmoil and economic shifts, the call for sustainable practices has never been louder. We stand on the shoulders of giants who have paved the way with innovative ideas, resilient strategies, and indomitable spirits. Now, it's our turn to continue this transformation, armed with the power of knowledge and the courage to act.

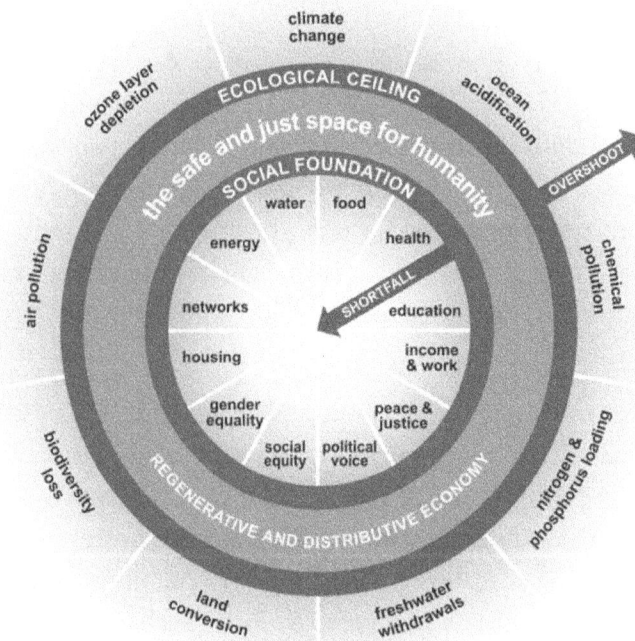

climate change
ozone layer depletion
ECOLOGICAL CEILING
ocean acidification
the safe and just space for humanity
SOCIAL FOUNDATION
water food
OVERSHOOT
air pollution
energy health
chemical pollution
networks SHORTFALL education
housing income & work
gender equality peace & justice
biodiversity loss
social equity political voice
REGENERATIVE AND DISTRIBUTIVE ECONOMY
nitrogen & phosphorus loading
land conversion
freshwater withdrawals

Set against the backdrop of historical contexts and evolving economic landscapes, the urgency to align business strategies with sustainable principles becomes glaringly evident. This book will navigate through the annals of time, illustrating how past choices shape our present and influence our future. We won't dwell on laurels but will instead focus on actionable pathways that lead to tangible results.

The case for sustainability isn't just a moral imperative; it's a lucrative endeavour. Companies that have invested in green technologies, embraced sustainable business models, and adhered to ethical guidelines have not only thrived but also set new benchmarks in profitability and competitiveness. You'll see real-life examples of businesses that transformed their operations and, in return, reaped significant financial and social benefits.

Finance isn't just the backbone of business; it's the lifeblood of sustainable transformation. By exploring the realm of sustainable investing, this book will shed light on the financial instruments and mechanisms designed to drive ecological progress. From green bonds to impact investing, the financial landscape is teeming with tools that can catapult us toward a more sustainable future.

Corporate strategy needs a paradigm shift. The integration of sustainability into core business operations is not a choice but a necessity. This foreword is here to plant the seed of curiosity about the subsequent chapters that delve into strategic steps, leadership roles, and governance models pivotal for embedding sustainability deep within the corporate DNA.

Numbers tell a story, metrics give it clarity. Measuring sustainability efforts through Key Performance Indicators (KPIs) and adhering to global reporting standards shifts abstract goals into concrete realities. This book will navigate through these necessary metrics, offering guidance on how to measure what truly matters.

Innovation and shifting towards green technologies form the bedrock of sustainable transformation. Research and Development for sustainable solutions propels us towards a future where resource efficiency and environmental stewardship are the norms, not the exceptions.

The journey won't be without its risks. Identifying and mitigating those risks, and building resilience in business operations, are crucial. Risk management isn't about fear; it's about foresight. It's about preparing for eventualities while seizing opportunities for growth.

Policy and regulation often cast long shadows over the business landscape. Understanding these regulations and actively engaging with policymakers can turn these challenges into growth catalysts. We're called to play an active role in shaping legislation that fosters sustainable practices rather than stifles innovation.

Stakeholder engagement and communication act as crucial links in the chain of sustainability. Identifying, understanding, and engaging with key stakeholders reinforces trust and cooperation. An effective communication strategy ensures that the message of sustainability resonates far and wide.

Financing sustainable projects is a vital cog in the wheel of transformation. Accessing capital, leveraging the role of banks and financial institutions, and exploring new financing models can bridge the gap between vision and reality.

The impact of sustainable practices on human capital cannot be understated. Retaining and developing quality jobs, investing in training and education for a green economy, and fostering a culture of sustainability within the workforce are essential for enduring success.

As we set the stage for this transformative journey, remember that the road to sustainability is paved with intention, innovation, and resilience. This book is not just a repository of knowledge; it's a catalyst for action, a guide for equipping you with the tools necessary to spearhead sustainable transformation in your professional arena.

Embark on this journey with curiosity and determination. The pursuit of sustainable transformation is not just a professional obligation; it's a moral duty. Let's step into this new dawn with hearts full of hope and minds geared for change. The stage is set; it's time to act.

To help you with this journey, I've put together a scorecard that will take stock of your life, study, work, buying and investing behaviour. Please <u>click here</u>, to let me know who you are, so that we can keep in touch.

Introduction:
The Concept of Eco-Economics

In a world where environmental degradation and economic disparity often sit side by side, a new paradigm is emerging—eco-economics. This isn't just another buzzword or an abstract theory circulating within academic circles. It's a robust framework, a strategic blend that reconciles the seemingly disparate goals of economic growth and environmental sustainability. For the mid-career professional, especially those with a grounding in finance and investing, understanding eco-economics is like finding a powerful compass in the treacherous waters of global markets and resource management.

Eco-economics is underpinned by one fundamental premise: economic systems must operate within the earth's ecological limits. Simple as that sounds, the implementation is a complex dance of economics, environmental science, policy, and societal behaviour. Imagine a financial system that not only thrives on profit but ensures the longevity of the planet's ecosystems—blueprints of forests, oceans, and the biosphere ingrained in every business decision.

This concept transcends the traditional boundaries of economic thought and business strategies. It requires us to rethink and rebuild the conventional models of growth that have long ignored their environmental footprints. We're moving from linear thinking—where products are made, used, and discarded—to a circular economy where waste becomes a resource, and sustainability is the default rather than the alternative.

The potential of eco-economics lies in its integrative approach. It brings together diverse disciplines, from finance to biology, from sociology to technology. The aim isn't merely to lessen the environmental impact but to create systems where prosperity and planetary health go hand in hand. It's an ambitious shift, demanding more than institutional changes. It calls for a transformation in our collective mindset, reshaping our values and redefining progress.

In the world of investment, this concept takes a bold stance. Eco-economics encourages a pivot from short-term gains to long-term value creation. Imagine portfolios that not only perform well on the balance sheets but also contribute to the regeneration of forests, the reduction of carbon footprints, and the promotion of social equity. As stewards of capital, you aren't just observers; you're participants in a movement that holds the potential to reshape markets and societies alike.

For businesses, embedding eco-economics isn't just about adopting green policies. It's about systemic change—integrating sustainability into the core of strategic planning and daily operations. This includes using renewable resources, minimising waste, and adopting new business models that prioritise ecological and social outcomes alongside financial results. The challenge lies in execution, in transforming bold visions into tangible actions that make economic sense and foster environmental integrity.

Now, cast your eyes on the evolving financial landscape. The era of sustainable investing is upon us, driven by a growing understanding that environmental, social, and governance (ESG) criteria are integral to assessing a company's long-term viability. Larger markets recognise the financial value in sustainability, leading to innovations in financial instruments and mechanisms. Green bonds, impact investing, and ESG integration aren't just trends—they're becoming foundational elements in modern finance.

Leadership plays a decisive role in this journey. As change agents, leaders need to articulate a vision that fuses economic and environmental goals, inspiring their teams and stakeholders to embrace sustainable practices. True leadership is about navigating uncertainties, fostering a culture of innovation, and maintaining a steadfast commitment to sustainability, even when immediate returns aren't apparent.

Metrics and measurements are critical in this transformation. Defining clear key performance indicators (KPIs) that reflect eco-economic goals ensures accountability and progress. But beyond numbers and data, it's about delivering a transparent narrative that communicates the broader impact—how every action taken today contributes to a resilient, sustainable future.

Innovation is the lifeblood of eco-economics. Advancements in green tech, coupled with relentless research and development, drive us towards solutions that mitigate environmental damage and create new economic opportunities. Creativity and scientific prowess converge, leading to breakthroughs that redefine industries and reset benchmarks for sustainability.

Risk management emerges as a pivotal factor. Identifying and mitigating risks in a sustainable context involves grasping the multifaceted environmental impacts and incorporating resilience into every aspect of business operations. It's about planning for contingencies, adapting to changes, and ensuring that businesses are future-proofed against ecological uncertainties.

Policy and regulation form the backdrop against which eco-economics unfolds. Engaging with policymakers to frame supportive regulations isn't just desirable—it's essential. This collaborative interplay between businesses and governments ensures that the frameworks governing economic activities align with ecological imperatives.

Effective stakeholder engagement and communication amplify the impact of eco-economics. Identifying key stakeholders and crafting strategies to communicate the sustainable vision fosters inclusivity and collective action. Businesses, consumers, governments, and communities must come together, united by a shared commitment to sustainability.

The concept of eco-economics invites us to rethink, restructure, and redefine. It stretches beyond the realms of possibility into the realm of necessity. As we delve deeper into this exploration, we'll unveil tools, strategies, and metrics that bring the vision of a sustainable economy into sharp focus. Each chapter ahead will serve as a stepping stone on this transformative journey, a journey not just of economic growth, but of harmonious coexistence with our planet.

Welcome to the concept of eco-economics. It's more than a vision—it's the roadmap for a sustainable, prosperous, and resilient future.

Preface:
Understanding Eco-Economics

Imagine a future where every financial decision aligns seamlessly with environmental sustainability, where profit and planet walk hand-in-hand. That's the vision driving this book. In a world increasingly strained by environmental challenges, the concept of eco-economics emerges as a beacon of hope and a pathway to sustainable transformation.

As mid-career professionals with a foundation in finance and investing, you're well aware of how traditional economics operates. What we're embarking on here is a reimagining of that very framework. Eco-economics isn't just an academic exercise; it's a call to action to reshape how we think about and interact with the financial world.

The need for this shift has never been more urgent. Climate change, resource depletion, and social inequities demand new economic models capable of fostering long-term, sustainable growth. Our current trajectory isn't just unsustainable; it's perilous. Eco-economics provides the tools and perspectives needed to navigate and transform this landscape.

Eco-economics is more than a buzzword. It's a comprehensive approach that integrates environmental and social considerations into economic decision-making. It challenges the status quo, questioning the relentless pursuit of growth for growth's sake and emphasising value that need not come at the expense of our planet.

Initially, the scope of eco-economics might seem daunting, but it's fundamentally about reconciling three perspectives: economic prosperity, social equity, and environmental integrity. These pillars don't exist in isolation. They are deeply interconnected and reinforcing, creating a robust framework for thinking about the future.

You might wonder, "Why now?" The reality is that change is being driven by a combination of growing environmental awareness, increasingly stringent regulatory landscapes, and shifting consumer demands. These forces are compelling businesses and investors to overhaul their strategies, investing not just in financial returns but in sustainable futures.

Your expertise in finance provides a unique vantage point. You understand the language of balance sheets and profit margins, but eco-economics asks you to expand this lexicon. It's not about abandoning financial performance metrics but rather enhancing them to include environmental and social impacts. This comprehensive view not only reduces risks but unveils new opportunities for innovation and growth.

Think of the marketplace as a dynamic ecology, where each entity—whether a company, an investor, or a policymaker—plays a vital role. In this ecosystem, the health of one directly impacts the others. By adopting eco-economic principles, we ensure that this ecosystem thrives holistically rather than at the expense of one of its parts.

In navigating eco-economics, we must also confront the myths that suggest sustainable practices are synonymous with reduced profitability. On the contrary, firms that integrate sustainability into their core strategies often outperform their peers in the long run. These companies innovate, attract talent, and develop resilient operations that weather economic and environmental storms.

One might question the tangibility of these ideas. How can abstract principles translate into actionable strategies? Throughout this book, we'll break down these high-level concepts into practical steps tailored for various stakeholders, including businesses, investors, and policymakers. We'll delve into case studies, uncover key financial instruments, and explore metrics that genuinely matter.

The power of eco-economics lies in its potential to redefine success. Instead of viewing economic, environmental, and social goals as competing interests, eco-economics aligns them. This alignment isn't just possible—it's profitable, prudent, and imperative.

Our journey into eco-economics will reveal how innovation, backed by sustainable practices, creates lasting value. We'll explore the role of leadership and governance in steering this transformation, showing that the shift towards sustainability extends beyond boardrooms and affects every layer of an organisation.

As we lay the groundwork for understanding eco-economics, keep in mind that this isn't merely an academic pursuit. It's a transformative outlook that should inspire immediate and tangible action. The aim is to equip you with the knowledge and tools needed to champion this change within your own spheres of influence.

This preface sets the stage for an exploration that's as intellectual as it is actionable. We're not just theorising; we're laying out a strategic pathway to a future where economic activity nurtures the planet rather than depleting it. The subsequent chapters will expand on these ideas, offering deeper insights and practical guidelines tailored to your expertise and aspirations.

In closing, eco-economics serves as both a mirror and a map—a reflection of our current state and a guide to where we need to go. The stakes are high and the journey demanding, but the benefits—lasting prosperity, social equity, and a sustainable planet—are well worth the effort. Let's set forth not just to understand eco-economics, but to embody and advance its principles.

Chapter 1:
Historical Context and Evolution

In order to understand the present drive for sustainable transformation, it's essential to take a step back and look at how we got here. The journey's been long, marked by significant shifts in thought and practice. Who could have imagined that what started as simple subsistence would one day culminate in an urgent call for sustainable practices across all sectors of society? The seeds of our current eco-consciousness were sown long ago, and tracing their evolution can offer valuable insights into where we go from here.

Human interaction with the environment initially revolved around survival. Early agricultural practices, for instance, were driven by necessity rather than any concept of sustainability. Nomadic tribes transitioned into settled agricultural communities, and with that came the first incidences of environmental manipulation. Clear forests, harness the water, cultivate the land—and repeat. The focus lay squarely on productivity, with little thought given to the long-term impacts on the ecosystem.

The Industrial Revolution, spanning the late 18th to early 19th century, marked a monumental shift. It was a time of unprecedented technological advancement that transformed society. Factories sprang up, cities expanded, and production skyrocketed. But along with prosperity came pollution, deforestation, and a relentless strain on natural resources. The drive for economic growth overshadowed environmental concerns, creating a legacy of damage that we're still grappling with today.

As the 20th century unfolded, initially, environmental issues took a backseat to economic development and industrial growth. But even during these times, moments of environmental awakening began to surface. The Dust Bowl of the 1930s in the United States, for example, underscored the harsh reality of environmental degradation caused by poor agricultural practices. These lessons proved costly but were often ignored in the broader drive towards more and greater production.

Post-World War II, the advent of consumer culture added another layer of complexity. Rapid urbanisation, increased consumerism, and the development of plastics revolutionised lifestyles but also ushered in a new era of waste and environmental negligence. It wasn't until the 1960s and 70s that the tide began to turn, driven by a growing awareness of the ecological harms perpetuated by unchecked industrial activity.

The publication of Rachel Carson's "Silent Spring" in 1962 is often cited as a pivotal moment. Carson's work illuminated the damaging impacts of pesticides on wildlife and ecosystems, laying bare the interconnectedness of human actions and the environment. This period saw the emergence of environmental movements across the globe, advocating for policies that took ecological health into account.

The 1980s and 1990s saw a shift in perspective, propelled by increasing evidence of climate change and widespread ecological degradation. Reports like the Brundtland Report of 1987, formally known as "Our Common Future," brought the concept of "sustainable development" into the mainstream lexicon. The report articulated the need for development that meets the needs of the present without compromising the ability of future generations to meet their own needs.

The Rio Earth Summit of 1992 set the stage for international cooperation on environmental issues. This gathering of world leaders resulted in landmark agreements on climate change, biodiversity, and sustainable development. It reflected a growing consensus that economic growth could no longer be pursued at the expense of environmental health.

In the early 21st century, the focus shifted from raising awareness to taking action. Al Gore's "An Inconvenient Truth," released in 2006, brought the issue of climate change into everyday conversation. Around the same time, businesses began to see the value proposition in sustainability. Green technologies, renewable energy sources, and sustainable business practices started gaining traction.

Regulatory frameworks also began to evolve. Governments worldwide started implementing stricter regulations to curb emissions, protect natural habitats, and promote sustainable practices. This regulatory push not only underscored the seriousness of climate issues but also highlighted the role that policy could play in steering economic activities towards more sustainable pathways.

Modern corporate strategies increasingly incorporate sustainability, not as an afterthought but as a core principle. Brands began to realise that sustainability can drive innovation, create new market opportunities, and build stronger relationships with consumers. Environmental, Social, and Governance (ESG) criteria became critical metrics for investors, reflecting a growing recognition that a company's long-term viability is intertwined with its environmental and social impact.

Yet, the road has been anything but straightforward. Each step towards greater environmental consciousness met resistance and challenges. Entrenched economic interests, lack of technological solutions, and geopolitical complexities have all posed significant hurdles. But these obstacles also spurred innovation and collaboration, leading to some of the most transformative initiatives we see today.

At its core, the push for sustainable transformation reflects a fundamental shift in how we view our place in the world. We're moving away from a mindset of exploitation towards one of stewardship. This change is not just driven by a sense of responsibility but also by a recognition that sustainability is crucial for our own survival and prosperity.

The historical context of our ecological footprint reveals a lot about human priorities and values over time. As we move forward, it's clear that embracing sustainability isn't just a necessity; it's an opportunity. An opportunity to innovate, to build resilient economies, to foster communities, and to create a future where both human and environmental health thrive.

The road ahead will require commitment, innovation, and above all, a willingness to change. As you delve deeper into the following chapters, remember that understanding our past is essential for shaping a sustainable future. The evolution of our relationship with the environment serves not only as a guide but as a beacon, lighting the way towards a more equitable and sustainable world.

Chapter 2:
The Business Case for Sustainability

Pondering the evolution of business over the last few decades, it's evident how traditional models focused narrowly on profit maximisation. This narrow lens is now revealing its limitations, as environmental and social costs of doing business are becoming glaringly unsustainable. Today's business leaders are embracing a broader view, realising that sustainability is not just a trend but a fundamental shift in how companies can thrive.

Embedding sustainability into the core operations is no longer a matter of choice but of competitive necessity. Companies that adopt sustainable practices are not merely improving their public image; they're also securing long-term profitability and survival. In fiercely competitive markets, the unique value propositions derived from sustainable practices often translate into significant competitive advantages. It's a simple yet profound truth — sustainability is good for the bottom line.

Consider profitability. Sustainable companies often become magnets for investments as more investors are inclined toward supporting businesses that demonstrate responsible practices. The rise of ESG (Environmental, Social, Governance) investing is a testament to this changing tide. Investors aren't just looking for short-term gains anymore; they are also seeking companies that promise sustainable returns over the long run. Thus, adopting sustainability can broaden access to capital and attract patient investors.

Competitiveness, on the other hand, hinges on innovation and adaptability. Sustainable practices foster innovation, pushing companies to rethink traditional approaches and embrace new technologies that reduce waste, increase efficiency, and lower costs. These adaptations allow companies to stay agile and competitive in rapidly changing markets. Progressive companies are those that foresee and adapt to changes, outpacing those stuck in conventional models.

A glance at successful businesses underscores this truth. Patagonia, a beacon of sustainability, has not only built a loyal customer base but also set benchmarks for environmental responsibility. The company's profits have consistently soared, showing us that prioritising the planet can also fatten wallets. Similarly, Unilever's focus on sustainable living brands has driven growth, proving that you can do well by doing good.

Moreover, an emphasis on sustainability can shore up a business against potential risks. Environmental regulations are tightening globally, and companies lagging in sustainability could face heavy fines, legal action, or even bans from certain markets. Conversely, proactive businesses aligning their operations with forthcoming regulations are naturally more resilient. They mitigate risks before they become financial burdens.

Let's turn our attention to operational efficiencies. Sustainable practices often result in leaner, more efficient operations. Take the circular economy model, for instance — recycling materials, reusing components, and reducing waste can all lead to cost savings. In manufacturing, energy-efficient processes can cut down utility bills substantially. Each small step toward sustainability accumulates, resulting in considerable cost advantages.

Customer loyalty also finds a firm ally in sustainability. Consumers today are more informed and concerned about the environmental and ethical footprint of their purchases. Companies prioritising transparency and sustainable practices are more likely to earn and retain customer loyalty. This allegiance isn't just good for sales; it strengthens brand reputation and enhances long-term viability.

The human capital aspect can't be ignored either. Companies known for their sustainability efforts are often preferred employers. They attract and retain talent looking for purpose-driven careers. Employee engagement and morale improve when individuals feel aligned with their organisation's values, driving productivity and innovation. This synergy between corporate and personal values can be a powerful engine for growth.

In conclusion, the business case for sustainability is compelling. It's about leveraging sustainability for profitability, competitive advantage, risk management, operational efficiency, and strong stakeholder relationships. Forward-thinking companies understand that the path to long-term success is paved with sustainable practices. The opportunity is immense; it's time to seize it.

Profitability and Competitiveness

In the current economic climate, the bedrock of any business's success hinges on its ability to generate profit and remain competitive. Yet, as we step into a new era of sustainability, these traditional measures of success are being redefined. Embracing sustainability doesn't just tick a box for corporate social responsibility; it shapes the core strategy that future-proofs businesses.

Sustainable practices offer profound cost-saving opportunities. Consider the reduction in energy consumption through improved efficiency, or the minimisation of waste. These aren't mere tweaks but transformational shifts that slash operational costs. Companies can see tangible financial benefits as soon as they integrate sustainable technologies, such as renewable energy sources and energy-efficient machinery. This immediate cost reduction becomes a compelling argument for businesses evaluating their sustainability roadmap.

Moreover, sustainability is a gateway to innovation. Businesses that innovate in the realm of sustainable products or services create new markets and revenue streams. Not only does this bolster profitability, but it also propels companies ahead of competitors who cling to conventional methods. Firms that lead in sustainability are often seen as pioneers, attracting customers who prefer to support forward-thinking brands.

The competitive landscape is also evolving. Consumers, investors, and partners are increasingly leaning towards businesses that demonstrate a genuine commitment to environmental and social governance (ESG) criteria. This shift means that companies with strong sustainability credentials are positioned favourably in the market. They attract more discerning customers, enjoy higher brand loyalty, and can even command premium pricing.

Additionally, sustainable businesses benefit from a reputational halo effect. In an age where information flows freely, and transparency is valued, a sustainable reputation can differentiate a business from its competitors. This reputational capital translates into trust, which is particularly crucial in maintaining market share and expanding into new arenas. The trustworthiness that stems from ethical practices can't be bought; it must be earned and sustained over time.

Beyond consumer preferences, sustainability enhances a company's appeal to investors. ESG investing is no longer a niche; it's gaining traction across mainstream financial markets. Investors recognise that businesses entrenched in sustainable practices are less likely to suffer from regulatory penalties or reputational damage. For companies, this translates into easier access to capital and potentially lower borrowing costs.

Considering the regulatory environment, early adopters of sustainable practices stay ahead of impending regulations. They avoid costly compliance issues and potential fines, thus safeguarding their financial health. More than just defensive posturing, this proactive approach signals to the market that a business is resilient and well-prepared for future shifts in legislation and market demand.

Another critical aspect is talent acquisition and retention. Today's workforce is increasingly value-driven, desiring to work for companies that align with their personal ethos. Companies with robust sustainability strategies attract and retain top-tier talent, fostering a motivated and innovative workforce. This not only boosts productivity but also reduces costs related to high turnover rates.

Entrepreneurial ventures, particularly start-ups, find sustainability to be a compelling differentiator. In crowded markets, sustainable practices help new businesses stand out, drawing attention from investors, consumers, and partners alike. These ventures often display agility, enabling them to implement sustainable innovations faster than established corporations burdened by legacy systems.

Small and medium-sized enterprises (SMEs) aren't left out either. Although they might operate on tighter budgets than large corporations, sustainable practices can offer them competitive advantages in niche markets. By leveraging local resources and minimising environmental impact, SMEs often build strong community ties, which in turn fosters loyalty and provides stable market foundations.

What about large, established corporations? Integrating sustainability at scale redefines their operational paradigms. These corporations wield significant influence and resources, allowing them to drive substantial change. As industry leaders, their commitment to sustainability sets industry benchmarks and influences entire supply chains.

Speaking of supply chains, sustainable practices entail a more ethical and transparent supply chain management. This ensures fair labour practices, equitable material sourcing, and environmentally friendly logistics. Transparent supply chains not only minimise risks but also align with the growing consumer demand for ethical products.

Moreover, sustainability reports and disclosures are not just for compliance; they're strategic tools. Businesses that regularly disclose their sustainability performance through comprehensive reporting demonstrate accountability. This doesn't only fulfil stakeholder expectations but also drives continuous improvement as companies strive to meet or exceed their sustainability goals.

While initial investments in sustainability can be substantial, viewing these expenditures as long-term investments is crucial. The return on investment (ROI) spans beyond immediate financial gains to include intangible benefits such as brand equity, customer loyalty, and market positioning. Sustainable investments fortify a company's foundation, ensuring it remains competitive in an unpredictable market.

Sustainability isn't a zero-sum game. It creates a competitive edge while delivering profitability and growth. A business's endeavour towards sustainability moulds a resilient, innovative, and forward-thinking enterprise. As the narrative unfolds, it becomes clear that the path to sustained profitability and competitiveness in today's marketplace is inextricably linked with sustainable business practices.

Case Studies of Successful Companies

When discussing the business case for sustainability, it's crucial to showcase companies that've not only embraced sustainability but also achieved remarkable success through it. These organisations have navigated the turbulent waters of eco-economics, emerging stronger, more profitable, and undeniably competitive. Their stories serve as powerful illustrations of the immense potential within sustainable business practices.

One of the most lauded examples is **Unilever**. With their Sustainable Living Plan launched in 2010, they set ambitious targets for reducing their environmental footprint while enhancing social impact. The key takeaway here is how sustainability became the cornerstone of their business strategy. Unilever reported that their sustainable living brands grew 69% faster than the rest of their business, accounting for 75% of the company's overall growth. This demonstrates that eco-friendly initiatives can drive significant revenue.

Another compelling story comes from **Patagonia**. This outdoor apparel giant has long been a beacon for sustainable practices. Patagonia's commitment goes beyond mere corporate social responsibility; it's embedded in their DNA. They've committed to sourcing materials responsibly, engaging in fair labour practices, and taking a recycling-first approach to their products. Remarkably, Patagonia chose to prioritise the environment over sheer profit. This approach hasn't deterred customers; instead, it's cultivated a loyal, almost evangelical customer base that values the company's principles. Patagonia's revenue has seen consistent growth, proving that a deep commitment to sustainability can strengthen brand loyalty and expand the market.

The tech sector also offers noteworthy examples. Consider **Google**. The tech giant has been carbon-neutral since 2007, and in 2017, it became the first major company to match 100% of its electricity consumption with renewable energy. Through extensive investments in wind and solar power, Google isn't just reducing its environmental footprint; it's also future-proofing its operations against energy price volatility. By significantly decreasing operational costs and ensuring a steady energy supply, Google illustrates that renewable investment can result in both economic and environmental dividends.

IKEA provides another case that combining sustainability with profitability can yield substantial results. The Swedish furniture behemoth has invested heavily in renewable energy, aiming to become climate positive by 2030. Additionally, their initiatives for converting waste into resources and promoting sustainable living at home resonate loudly with their customer base. IKEA has not only enhanced its brand image but also driven down operational costs and developed new revenue streams through recycling programmes.

Then there's **Tesla**, the company that revolutionised the automotive industry. By leading the charge toward electric vehicles and sustainable energy solutions, Tesla's market valuation has soared, making it one of the most valuable companies globally. Tesla's success story is not merely about cars; it's about establishing an energy ecosystem encompassing solar energy, battery storage, and electric mobility. Through relentless innovation and a clear vision of sustainability, Tesla has turned scepticism into sky-high stock prices.

General Electric (GE) also deserves a mention. Once primarily known for traditional energy production, GE pivoted towards sustainability with its Ecomagination initiative. This strategy focuses on delivering cleaner and more efficient technologies across various sectors. The results? Increased market share, substantial R&D advancements, and a favourable public image. Ecomagination has raked in billions in revenue, signifying how a legacy company can successfully pivot to embrace green technology.

Nike, too, has an inspiring narrative. Through its "Move to Zero" campaign, Nike aims to reduce carbon emissions to zero and eliminate waste from its supply chain. They've embraced renewable energy sources and material innovation, shifting towards recycled content. This sustainable commitment hasn't just boosted their environmental credentials; it's also driven significant cost savings and innovation.

One more remarkable case study stems from the automotive sector: **BMW**. BMW's i-series range of electric cars showcases their commitment to sustainability and innovation. Investments in battery technology, lightweight materials, and renewable energy for their plants have positioned BMW as a frontrunner in sustainable mobility. Their i-series has been commercially successful and helped solidify their standing as an eco-conscious luxury brand.

Starbucks also offers valuable lessons. The global coffeehouse chain has embraced sustainability through ethical sourcing, waste reduction, and green building initiatives. Starbucks has focused on creating a positive impact on the farming communities they source from, which resonates positively with their customer base. This approach hasn't just built goodwill but also ensured a sustainable supply chain, driving long-term business stability.

Interface, a global leader in modular flooring, is another stellar example of sustainability-driven success. Their Mission Zero goal aims to eliminate any negative environmental impact by 2020. Through radical innovation and commitment, Interface has seen reduced costs through waste minimisation and energy efficiency. Their strong sustainability credentials have not only attracted clientele but also top talent who wish to be part of a purpose-driven organisation.

Likewise, **Siemens** showcases how a diversified approach to sustainability can yield significant returns. Siemens invested substantially in renewable energy projects and green technologies. This shift has led to numerous energy-efficient solutions across various industries, propelling Siemens into a leadership position in the global green technology market. Their case demonstrates that sustainability can be a strategic lever for business expansion and technological leadership.

Then there's **Apple**. Renowned for its sleek designs and cutting-edge technology, Apple has also made significant strides in sustainability. From committing to using 100% recycled materials in products to achieving zero waste in many of its supply chains, Apple exemplifies how large corporations can drive substantial environmental impact. Their concerted efforts have not only bolstered their marketing campaigns but also streamlined their material costs and fortified their public image.

Retail giant **Walmart** has also made strides in sustainability, focusing on renewable energy and waste reduction. By setting the ambitious goal of achieving zero waste across its U.S. operations by 2025 and reducing greenhouse gas emissions from its supply chain, Walmart has cut operational costs and developed a more resilient supply chain. Their sustainable practices have led to both economic and reputational benefits, capturing the attention of environmentally conscious consumers.

Last, but certainly not least, is **Danone**, the multinational food-products corporation. Danone's "One Planet. One Health" sustainability framework focuses on health and sustainability as interconnected goals. By prioritising organic farming, reducing water usage, and committing to carbon neutrality, Danone has built a robust, sustainable business model. These endeavours have not only contributed to environmental health but have also driven substantial consumer trust and loyalty.

These case studies illustrate that sustainability and profitability are not mutually exclusive but rather complementary. In each instance, these companies have shown that sustainable practices can drive significant market differentiation, cost savings, and long-term viability. Their journeys are beacons of inspiration for all businesses striving to integrate sustainable strategies. They remind us that the path to sustainability, though challenging, is paved with opportunities for innovation, growth, and lasting impact.

Chapter 3:
The Financial Landscape of
Sustainability

In assessing the transformative journey towards sustainability, one must first navigate the complex terrain of the financial landscape. This landscape is characterised by a dynamic interplay between traditional financial systems and emergent sustainable investing practices. At its core, sustainability within finance isn't merely about mitigating risk; it's about identifying opportunities that align profit with purpose. Once considered a niche market, sustainable investing now stands at the forefront of strategic financial planning, driving significant capital flow towards green ventures.

Over the past decade, the financial sector has witnessed substantial growth in sustainable investment funds, both in terms of assets under management and the diversity of financial instruments available. From green bonds to impact investing, these mechanisms provide investors with more avenues to channel funds into socially responsible and environmentally beneficial projects. Instruments such as Environmental, Social, and Governance (ESG) benchmarks are becoming pivotal. They guide investors in aligning their portfolios with broader ecological and social objectives. This marks a shift from the old paradigm where financial returns were pursued with little regard for their environmental and social costs.

The financial landscape of sustainability is not without its challenges, yet the opportunities are immense. For mid-career

28

professionals, understanding and navigating this evolving field is critical. It demands both knowledge and a keen sense of the ethical imperatives that underpin today's investment decisions. In this new chapter, financial professionals must become adept at balancing short-term returns with long-term sustainability goals. Investment strategies that embrace this dual focus will not only contribute to a healthier planet but also generate robust financial outcomes. The era of sustainable finance is here; it calls for a reimagination of economic prosperity, where success is measured not only by earnings but by the positive impact on our world.

Sustainable Investing: An Overview

In the context of a world increasingly aware of its finite resources, sustainable investing arises not just as a trend but as a profound shift in financial paradigms. It's a recognition that the old ways of doing business — that often ignored the environmental and social costs — are no longer tenable. As mid-career professionals in finance, many of you are undoubtedly familiar with the core mechanics of investing. Yet, sustainable investing demands a broader perspective where financial returns intersect with environmental stewardship and social responsibility.

This is not merely a lofty ideal but a critical reconfiguration of how capital is allocated and grown. Sustainable investing, also known as ESG investing, integrates Environmental, Social, and Governance factors into investment decisions. This approach seeks not just monetary gains but also strives for positive environmental and social impacts, all the while ensuring robust governance practices. Think of this as a three-legged stool where each leg — environmental, social, and governance — must be strong enough to support enduring success.

Historically, investments prioritised profit margins, often sidelining ecological and social impacts. This led to practices that, while profitable in the short term, incurred significant costs in terms of environmental degradation and social inequity. Today, the narrative is shifting. Sustainable investing redefines the notion of "value" by encompassing long-term societal and environmental benefits.

The roots of sustainable investing are not newfound. Ethical investments can be traced back centuries, with religious groups avoiding investments in 'sin stocks' — companies associated with alcohol, tobacco, and gambling. The social movements of the 1960s and 1970s further pushed for investments that aligned with social justice, leading to the divestment from apartheid South Africa. However, sustainable investing as we know it today started to crystallise in the late 20th and early 21st centuries, driven by globalisation, climate awareness, and corporate scandals that underscored the importance of governance.

In psychological terms, investing sustainably is about aligning your financial footprint with your moral compass. While it's easy to be swayed by trends, sustainable investing is grounded in solid research and a deep understanding of the companies and projects being financed. A key aspect here is due diligence, ensuring that the companies claiming to be 'green' or 'socially responsible' truly meet the standards they profess. This involves scrutinising their supply chains, labour practices, and carbon footprints, among other things.

One can't ignore the performance aspect — a frequent concern among investors hesitant to pivot towards ESG-focused portfolios. Numerous studies have demonstrated that sustainable investments often perform on par with, or even better than, traditional investments. The reasoning is straightforward: companies that excel in ESG criteria are typically more resilient, better managed, and more attuned to risk factors that others might overlook. These factors contribute to their long-term profitability and stability.

However, the thrust of sustainable investing transcends the balance sheet. It encapsulates a broader vision where investing becomes a tool for societal transformation. When investors pour capital into renewable energy, affordable housing, or green technologies, they are directly contributing to solutions for some of the world's most pressing challenges. This is finance's higher calling — a way to wield capital as a force for good.

Presently, various financial products cater to the sustainable investing ethos. Green bonds, which fund environmentally friendly projects; sustainable mutual funds; and ESG-focused exchange-traded funds (ETFs) are some popular instruments. These financial products enable investors to diversify their portfolios while ensuring that their investments align with their ethical values. Moreover, impact investing goes a step further by targeting investments that yield explicit social or environmental benefits alongside financial returns.

Moreover, the role of technology in sustainable investing can't be overstated. Advanced analytics, blockchain, and artificial intelligence are transforming how investors assess ESG criteria, bringing unprecedented transparency and efficiency. For instance, blockchain can verify supply chain practices, ensuring they adhere to sustainability standards, while AI can analyse vast amounts of data to offer insights into a company's ESG performance.

Sustainable investing also necessitates a shift in corporate mindset. Businesses must move away from short-term profit maximisation to long-term value creation, embracing the idea that profit and purpose are not mutually exclusive. This shift often requires robust governance structures that can oversee the integration of ESG principles into core business strategies.

Companies that excel in this paradigm often find themselves rewarded by the markets. They attract dedicated investors, enjoy customer loyalty, and frequently become employers of choice. The halo effect of being a 'sustainable' company extends far beyond mere optics; it embeds into the company's brand, culture, and operational ethos.

Legislation and policy also play a pivotal role in shaping the sustainable investing landscape. Regulatory frameworks are increasingly demanding greater transparency and accountability from companies regarding their ESG practices. These regulations not only protect investors but also ensure that corporations remain committed to their sustainability pledges.

While the journey towards embedding sustainability in investing is fraught with challenges, it is a path worth treading. The initial hurdles often involve higher research costs, the need for specialised knowledge, and the challenge of separating genuinely sustainable options from those indulging in 'greenwashing'. Yet, these obstacles are surmountable with the right mindset and resources.

Looking ahead, sustainable investing is poised to become the mainstream rather than the exception. As global challenges such as climate change, social inequality, and resource scarcity become increasingly urgent, the role of sustainable investing will only grow in significance. It's not just about avoiding the downside; it's about proactively building a better future for all stakeholders involved.

The task at hand is clear: to redefine profitability and stewardship in harmony. As we continue our expedition through the financial landscape of sustainability, remember that sustainable investing is not merely a strategy; it's an imperative for our collective future — a future that demands our diligence, our courage, and our unwavering commitment to transformation.

Key Financial Instruments and Mechanisms

In the ever-evolving landscape of sustainability, the role of financial instruments and mechanisms cannot be overstated. These tools, often the lifeblood of modern economies, don't simply provide the fuel for growth; they steer the direction of that growth. As sustainability rises to become a central tenet of corporate and societal progress, the financial world has adapted, offering new instruments and mechanisms designed to ensure that economic advancement doesn't come at the planet's expense.

At the heart of this transformation are green bonds, a powerful tool designed to channel investment into sustainable projects. Issued by governments, financial institutions, and corporations, these bonds specifically aim to fund initiatives that offer environmental benefits. From renewable energy projects to sustainable infrastructure, green bonds signal a commitment to long-term ecological health. In recent years, we have witnessed a surge in these bonds, driven by an increasing recognition of the urgent need to address climate change and environmental degradation.

Likewise, sustainability-linked loans (SLLs) have emerged as a versatile instrument in the financial landscape. Unlike green bonds, which dictate the use of proceeds, SLLs tie the borrowing costs to the borrower's sustainability performance. By setting specific targets—be it reducing carbon emissions, improving water efficiency, or meeting other sustainability benchmarks—borrowers can benefit from reduced interest rates if they achieve their goals. This mechanism aligns financial performance with sustainability objectives, incentivising tangible improvements and fostering a deeper integration of eco-friendly practices in corporate strategies.

In the domain of equity, impact investing has garnered significant attention. Impact investors seek both financial returns and measurable environmental or social impact. This dual-objective approach challenges the traditional notion of investing purely for profit. Impact funds meticulously select companies that demonstrate not just strong financial health but also a commitment to sustainable practices.

Through these investments, capital flows to enterprises that prioritise responsible resource management, ethical labour practices, and community engagement, all while delivering financial returns.

Transition bonds are another crucial addition to the arsenal of financial instruments supporting sustainability. These bonds aim to assist high-emission industries in their transition towards more sustainable operations. While their proceeds may not exclusively fund 'green' projects, they support initiatives that pave the way for a lower-carbon future. For instance, a transition bond might finance the modification of a traditional energy plant to increase its efficiency or to incorporate alternative energy sources.

Insurance-linked securities (ILS) have also found a foothold in the sustainability space, particularly through catastrophe bonds ('cat bonds'). These instruments provide a financial mechanism to manage the risk of natural disasters, which are becoming more frequent and severe due to climate change. Cat bonds enable insurers to transfer risk to capital markets, thereby spreading the financial impact of catastrophic events. This spreading of risk is crucial for resilience and recovery, ensuring that resources are available for rebuilding and adaptation in the aftermath of disasters.

The adoption of environmental, social, and governance (ESG) criteria in investment decisions has shifted from a niche consideration to a mainstream imperative. ESG metrics provide a framework for evaluating companies on their performance in these critical areas, guiding investors in making informed choices that reflect their values and priorities. Robust ESG practices not only mitigate risks and enhance reputational value but also correlate with long-term financial performance, contradicting the outdated perception that sustainability and profitability are mutually exclusive.

Carbon markets represent a financial mechanism that directly addresses the challenge of reducing greenhouse gas emissions. These markets, which include cap-and-trade systems and carbon offsets, create financial incentives for companies to lower their carbon footprint. By assigning a monetary value to carbon emissions, they encourage innovative solutions and investments in cleaner technologies. Cap-and-trade systems set an overall limit on emissions and allow companies to buy and sell allowances, fostering a market-driven approach to emission reductions.

Microfinance, though traditionally associated with poverty alleviation, plays a vital role in sustainable development, especially in emerging markets. By providing small loans to underserved communities, microfinance institutions enable grassroots entrepreneurs to launch and expand sustainable businesses. These ventures, often focused on agriculture, renewable energy, and local crafts, contribute to economic development while promoting environmental stewardship and social equity.

Public-private partnerships (PPPs) have proven to be effective in mobilising resources for large-scale sustainability projects. These collaborations leverage the strengths of both sectors, combining public sector oversight and private sector efficiency. PPPs are instrumental in financing infrastructure projects such as sustainable transport systems, clean energy installations, and waste management facilities. Through risk-sharing and pooled expertise, they enable projects that might otherwise be too complex or costly for a single entity to undertake.

Social impact bonds (SIBs) offer an innovative way to address social and environmental challenges through performance-based investments. In a SIB arrangement, private investors fund initiatives that aim to achieve specific outcomes, such as reducing homelessness or improving educational attainment. If the project succeeds in delivering the agreed-upon results, the government or another backer repays the investors with a return. This results-based approach ensures that funding is tied to tangible impact, driving effective solutions to pressing issues.

Renewable energy certificates (RECs) and guarantees of origin (GOs) are mechanisms that facilitate the market for renewable energy. RECs and GOs certify that electricity has been generated from renewable sources, allowing companies and individuals to support green energy production indirectly. By purchasing these certificates, consumers can claim their use of renewable energy, fostering transparency and accountability in the energy sector.

Sustainability-oriented financial instruments don't only incentivise good practices but also penalise unsustainable ones. Climate risk assessments and scenario analysis, now integral parts of financial due diligence, guide investors and businesses in recognising and mitigating climate-related financial risks. By incorporating these assessments into their decision-making processes, organisations can better navigate the uncertainties of a rapidly changing climate, ensuring long-term viability and resilience.

The growing trend of divestment from fossil fuels signifies a clear stance against practices that exacerbate climate change. By withdrawing investments from companies engaged in coal, oil, and gas, institutions—ranging from pension funds to university endowments—send a powerful message. Divestment not only challenges the viability of unsustainable industries but also reallocates capital towards renewable energy and other sustainable sectors, accelerating the transition to a low-carbon economy.

Finally, blended finance leverages philanthropic and public funds to attract private sector investment in sustainable development. By de-risking investments through grants, concessional loans, and guarantees, blended finance structures make it more attractive for private investors to commit capital to high-impact projects. This approach is particularly effective in closing the funding gap for achieving the

United Nations Sustainable Development Goals (SDGs), creating shared value by aligning diverse financial flows towards a common purpose.

The intricate web of financial instruments and mechanisms we've explored offers a blueprint for channeling capital towards sustainability. These tools, each with its unique strengths, converge on a singular objective: to foster an economy where profitability and planetary well-being are not at odds but are inextricably linked. By embracing and innovating within this framework, we navigate the complex yet rewarding path towards a sustainable future, demonstrating that the true measure of progress lies not just in economic gain but in the legacy we leave behind.

Chapter 4:
Embedding Sustainability in Corporate Strategy

Every organisation stands at a crossroads, where they must act decisively to embed sustainability into the core of their operations. It's not just a trend; it's imperative for long-term success. Today, we delve into the strategies that mid-career professionals, particularly those well-versed in finance and investing, can employ to integrate sustainable practices into their corporate strategies. This chapter aims to inspire not only thought but concrete action.

Start by recognising that business as usual is no longer viable. Sustainability should no longer be an add-on or a peripheral concern. It needs to be woven into the fabric of your corporate strategy. Companies that have successfully embedded sustainability are already reaping the benefits, not just in terms of image but in profitability and resilience. However, integrating sustainability requires a multifaceted approach, beginning with a clear vision and commitment from the leadership team.

Leadership sets the tone. The role of the board and the C-suite is crucial in this transformation. Leaders need to articulate a vision that goes beyond quarterly earnings and takes into account environmental, social, and economic impacts. This vision must be communicated consistently and broadly, ensuring that all stakeholders understand and align with the sustainability objectives. It is in these moments that leaders are born, not from grand gestures but from steadfast commitment to a sustainable future.

Next, let's focus on governance structures. Embedding sustainability involves reshaping governance frameworks to support sustainable goals. This could mean establishing a dedicated sustainability committee within the board or integrating sustainability targets into executive compensation. Robust governance structures ensure accountability and drive performance. Consider that companies like Unilever and Patagonia have integrated these practices, leading to enhanced accountability and significant positive outcomes.

Once leadership and governance are aligned, the next step is to conduct a comprehensive sustainability assessment. This involves evaluating all aspects of your operations, identifying areas where sustainability practices can be improved, from supply chain management to energy usage. It's not just about mitigating adverse impacts but also uncovering opportunities for positive change. Transformative insights often come from unexpected quarters — an operations manager's suggestion, a supplier's innovation, or even feedback from customers.

Developing clear, actionable steps is paramount. Define your sustainability targets and ensure they are specific, measurable, achievable, relevant, and time-bound (SMART). It's not enough to have a vague commitment; precision in goals drives action. For instance, if reducing carbon footprint is a goal, break it down into actionable steps: switching to renewable energy sources, improving energy efficiency, or investing in carbon offset programmes.

Integration also means embedding sustainability into the company culture. Culture eats strategy for breakfast, they say. Sustainable policies need to be lived and breathed by every member of the organisation, from the janitor to the CEO. Training programmes, internal communication strategies, and employee engagement initiatives play a crucial role. Often, it's the small, everyday actions of employees that drive transformative change.

Additionally, collaboration and partnerships can amplify efforts. Engage with various stakeholders, including suppliers, customers, NGOs, and even competitors, to share best practices and drive collective action. Collaboration can lead to innovation and open up new avenues for sustainability that one company might not be able to achieve on its own. Remember, in the ecosystem of business, no entity is an island; partnerships are the bridges to collective success.

Lastly, continuous monitoring and evaluation are essential. Sustainability is not a set-and-forget task. Regularly assess progress against your goals and be prepared to pivot strategies as needed. Use data and analytics to drive decisions, and be transparent in your reporting to stakeholders. Transparency builds trust, and trust drives engagement and investment.

Embedding sustainability in corporate strategy is a journey, not a destination. It requires steadfast dedication, creativity, and an unwavering commitment to making the world a better place for future generations. By leveraging leadership, robust governance, precise goal-setting, cultural integration, collaborative efforts, and continuous improvement, companies can not only survive but thrive in a rapidly changing world.

Steps to Integrate Sustainability

Embedding sustainability into a corporate strategy isn't a mere checkbox exercise; it's a profound transformation that redefines the role of business in society. It starts with a shift in mindset, seeing beyond immediate profits and recognising the long-term value of sustainable practices. Here, we'll outline the steps to integrate sustainability effectively, with the aim to inspire action and make sustainability a core component of your business strategy.

1. Assess Current Impact: The journey begins with understanding your starting point. Conduct a thorough assessment of your company's current environmental, social, and economic impacts. This involves a detailed analysis of your operations, supply chain, and product lifecycle. Gather data on resource use, waste production, and carbon emissions. This initial audit provides a baseline against which future improvements can be measured.

2. Define Sustainability Goals: With a clear picture of your current impact, set specific, measurable, achievable, relevant, and time-bound (SMART) sustainability goals. These should align with broader sustainability frameworks such as the United Nations Sustainable Development Goals (SDGs). Whether it's reducing carbon emissions by a certain percentage, achieving zero waste, or improving community engagement, well-defined goals will guide your efforts.

3. Secure Leadership Commitment: The commitment from top management is crucial for the successful integration of sustainability. Leaders must not only endorse sustainability initiatives but also actively participate in and champion them. Incorporate sustainability into the company's vision and mission statements, reflecting its strategic importance. Leadership commitment ensures that sustainability is prioritised and resourced appropriately.

4. Engage Stakeholders: Sustainability is a collective endeavour. Engage with a broad range of stakeholders, including employees, customers, suppliers, and community members. Through dialogue and collaboration, you can gain insights, identify potential challenges, and foster a sense of ownership and accountability. Stakeholder engagement is essential for the development of a holistic and inclusive sustainability strategy.

5. Integrate into Core Business Processes: To embed sustainability into your corporate strategy, integrate it into your core business processes. This involves revisiting product design, procurement practices, manufacturing processes, and logistics. Implement eco-efficiency measures, adopt circular economy principles, and prioritise sustainable sourcing. This transformation should be reflected in every aspect of your business operations.

6. Develop a Sustainability Team: Form a dedicated sustainability team or department to drive and coordinate sustainability initiatives. This team should include members with diverse skills and backgrounds, capable of addressing the various dimensions of sustainability. The team's responsibilities include developing sustainability policies, monitoring progress, and fostering a culture of sustainability throughout the organisation.

7. Foster Innovation: Embrace innovation as a key driver of sustainability. Encourage research and development of sustainable technologies and practices. Innovation can lead to breakthrough solutions that reduce environmental impact, improve resource efficiency, and create new business opportunities. Invest in sustainable innovations that align with your strategic goals and can offer competitive advantages.

8. Measure and Report Progress: Regularly measure and report your sustainability performance. Establish key performance indicators (KPIs) that align with your sustainability goals and track them diligently. Transparent reporting, both internally and externally, builds trust and demonstrates your commitment to sustainability. Use recognised reporting frameworks, such as the Global Reporting Initiative (GRI) or the Carbon Disclosure Project (CDP), to ensure consistency and comparability.

9. Build Sustainability into Corporate Culture: Sustainability should become a core value embedded in your corporate culture. Educate and train employees at all levels about the importance of sustainability and their role in achieving the company's goals. Encourage sustainable behaviours and practices in the workplace.

Recognition and reward systems can be used to incentivise sustainable actions and reinforce the sustainability ethos.

10. Collaborate and Share Best Practices: Collaboration is key to accelerating sustainability. Partner with other organisations, industry groups, and non-profits to share knowledge, resources, and best practices. Participate in sustainability networks and initiatives that promote collective action. Collaborative efforts can amplify impact and drive systemic changes across industries and sectors.

11. Review and Adapt: The journey towards sustainability is dynamic and ongoing. Regularly review and adapt your sustainability strategy to address new challenges, opportunities, and insights. Stay informed about emerging trends, regulatory changes, and technological advancements. Continuous improvement ensures that your sustainability efforts remain relevant and effective.

12. Communicate Achievements: Celebrate and communicate your sustainability achievements widely. Share success stories, milestones, and impact reports with your stakeholders. Effective communication not only builds trust but also inspires others to take similar actions. Use various platforms—annual reports, social media, press releases—to highlight your commitment and progress.

13. Create Long-term Value: Ultimately, integrating sustainability into your corporate strategy is about creating long-term value for both the business and society. Sustainable practices can lead to cost savings, risk reduction, enhanced brand reputation, and new revenue streams. More importantly, they contribute to a healthier planet and a more equitable society. Recognise and articulate the broader value proposition of sustainability to reinforce its strategic importance.

14. Foster a Sustainability Mindset: Instilling a sustainability mindset across the organisation is critical. Encourage employees to think sustainably in their daily roles and decision-making processes. Provide continuous education and training to cultivate this mindset. A work environment that values sustainability leads to more innovative solutions and sustained commitment from the entire workforce.

15. Lead by Example: Companies that integrate sustainability successfully serve as role models in their industries. By demonstrating that sustainability and profitability can go hand in hand, you inspire other businesses to embark on their sustainability journeys. Leadership in sustainability isn't just about transforming your own business; it's about paving the way for a more sustainable future for all.

Integrating sustainability into corporate strategy requires dedication, collaboration, and an unwavering commitment to continuous improvement. With each step, you're not just building a more resilient and future-ready business; you're contributing to a sustainable world that benefits everyone. Let's take these steps, not just because they're good for business, but because they're the right thing to do for our planet and future generations.

Role of Leadership and Governance

When it comes to embedding sustainability within corporate strategy, leadership and governance play a pivotal role. They're not just about implementing policies but about creating a culture that prioritises sustainability. A company's leadership sets the tone from the top, and when leaders are committed to sustainable practices, their influence cascades down through all levels of the organisation.

Ineffective leadership can render even the most well-crafted sustainability plans useless. An inspiring leader doesn't merely issue mandates; they embody the principles of sustainability in their daily actions, decisions, and communications. This kind of leadership ignites a spark within the workforce, fostering a collective commitment towards sustainable goals.

Governance provides the framework within which these efforts are orchestrated. Strong governance structures ensure that sustainability initiatives are not just talked about but are systematically integrated into business operations. This involves the establishment of clear policies, accountability mechanisms, and continuous monitoring and reporting systems. In essence, governance transforms high-level sustainability goals into actionable, measurable outcomes.

One story that stands out involves Paul Polman, former CEO of Unilever. Under his leadership, Unilever launched the Sustainable Living Plan, which aimed to decouple the company's growth from its environmental footprint while increasing its positive social impact. Polman's commitment was evident; he challenged norms, took bold decisions, and remained steadfast even when faced with scepticism. His vision permeated through the organisation, demonstrating how leadership can steer a company toward sustainable success.

Governance in this context isn't just about compliance; it's about fostering an environment where sustainability is a core value. This includes establishing board-level sustainability committees, integrating sustainability into executive incentives, and embedding environmental and social criteria into decision-making processes. These steps ensure that sustainability is prioritised across all facets of the business, from strategic planning to day-to-day operations.

What stands out is the transformative power of transparency. When leaders and governance bodies embrace transparency—by openly sharing both successes and challenges—they build trust with stakeholders. This trust is crucial for the long-term viability of sustainability initiatives. Stakeholders who see a genuine commitment to sustainability are more likely to support and engage with the company, whether they are employees, investors, customers, or partners.

The integration of sustainability into corporate strategy requires not just any leadership, but visionary leadership that can see beyond the immediate horizon. This involves anticipating future trends, recognising the long-term benefits of sustainable practices, and being willing to invest in these despite short-term costs. Such a vision must be backed by a robust governance structure that aligns the organisation's goals, resources, and capabilities towards achieving these visionary targets.

Leaders are also responsible for fostering a culture of innovation, which is essential for sustainable transformation. This involves empowering teams to experiment with new ideas and technologies, even if they come with uncertainties. By doing so, leaders can stimulate the development of innovative solutions that drive sustainability performance and competitive advantage.

Governance mechanisms must also ensure that the company's sustainability efforts are inclusive and equitable. This means engaging with a diverse range of voices and perspectives, both within and outside the organisation. Inclusive governance leads to more comprehensive and effective sustainability strategies, which are more likely to gain broad-based support and deliver meaningful impact.

Examples abound where leadership and governance have taken centre stage in the sustainability arena. Tesla, under Elon Musk's leadership, has disrupted the auto industry by mainstreaming electric vehicles and renewable energy solutions. This was not just a technological innovation but a governance triumph, where the board and executive management aligned their strategic goals with sustainable development objectives.

It's also important to consider the role of governance in mitigating risks associated with sustainability initiatives. Effective governance practices help identify potential risks early, allowing companies to develop strategies to mitigate these risks before they become significant issues. This proactive approach can safeguard the company's sustainability investment and ensure long-term resilience.

Leadership in sustainability requires a blend of passion and pragmatism. Passion fuels the commitment and drive needed to push through challenges, while pragmatism ensures that sustainability initiatives are grounded in solid business principles and deliver tangible results. This balance is crucial for fostering genuine, lasting change within the organisation.

Moreover, governance needs to be adaptive and responsive to the rapidly evolving landscape of sustainability. This involves staying abreast of emerging trends, regulatory changes, and stakeholder expectations, and adjusting strategies and policies accordingly. Such adaptability is key to maintaining the relevance and effectiveness of the company's sustainability efforts.

In essence, sustainable transformation begins at the top but must permeate throughout the organisation. Leadership and governance are the twin pillars that support this transformation, providing the vision, structure, and accountability needed to embed sustainability into the corporate fabric. As you move forward in your careers, remember the power you hold as leaders and stewards of governance. Your actions and decisions can pave the way for a more sustainable and equitable world.

Transformative leadership and robust governance are not lofty ideals but practical necessities in the quest for sustainability. They are the catalysts that convert intention into action, ambition into achievement. Let your leadership inspire, your governance empower, and together, let's craft a future where business success and sustainability are inextricably linked.

Chapter 5:
Metrics and Measurement

We've journeyed through the historical context and the business imperatives driving sustainability. But how do we measure progress in such a nuanced and complex domain? Metrics and measurement are foundational, serving as both compass and odometer for enterprises striving toward sustainable transformation. Numbers don't lie, and in the realm of sustainability, they are the evidence of our promises fulfilled—or not.

To define what success looks like, we must establish Key Performance Indicators (KPIs) that resonate with our sustainable ambitions. Setting these metrics goes beyond simple carbon footprints or energy use. It entails a rigorous, holistic appraisal of social, environmental, and economic dimensions. Companies must adopt KPIs that capture the breadth of their impact—metrics that encompass waste management, water usage, supply chain integrity, and even employee well-being.

Reporting standards like the Global Reporting Initiative (GRI) and the Sustainability Accounting Standards Board (SASB) offer frameworks that bring consistency and transparency. These standards set the yardstick for truth in reporting, helping investors and other stakeholders sift through the noise. By adhering to these benchmarks, companies gain not only trust but also a clearer pathway to continuous improvement. The more robust and candid the reporting, the greater the potential for impactful change.

Adopting these metrics and standards is not merely an exercise in compliance. It is an act of commitment to transparency and accountability. Inspired by a deeper purpose, businesses can use these tools to reveal vulnerabilities and highlight strengths. Regular, unaudited internal reviews help diagnose weaknesses and recalibrate strategies, fostering a culture of perpetual learning and growth.

As we march forward, let us remember that metrics and measurement are not the end but the means. They guide us, frame our achievements, and expose our failings. In the grand scheme of sustainable transformation, metrics are the stepping stones, shaping our journey and ensuring every step aligns with our broader vision of a just, equitable, and thriving future.

Defining Key Performance Indicators (KPIs)

In the grand tapestry of sustainability, Key Performance Indicators (KPIs) serve as the decisive threads that help us weave a coherent narrative. A well-defined KPI provides a snapshot of success, guiding both strategy and daily operations. Without KPIs, the journey towards sustainability resembles sailing without a compass. They provide clarity, help operationalize goals, and keep organisations accountable.

The first step in defining KPIs is understanding that not all indicators are created equal. Business leaders often grapple with choosing the right metrics that align with both economic and environmental priorities. KPIs should not be arbitrary but should emerge from a comprehensive assessment of what truly impacts both the bottom line and sustainability targets. This makes the exercise of defining KPIs more than a corporate ritual—it's a strategic imperative.

Context is crucial. What works for one industry might not be applicable to another. For instance, energy consumption per unit of output might be a critical KPI for manufacturing, whereas for a tech company, data centre efficiency might take precedence. The pivotal question here is: What are the most pressing sustainability issues that your business can influence? Addressing this question will help in narrowing down the vast array of potential indicators to those that matter the most.

Effective KPIs exhibit certain characteristics—they are Specific, Measurable, Achievable, Relevant, and Time-bound (SMART). Being specific means the KPI should clearly define what is being measured. Measurability involves setting a quantitative or qualitative benchmark. Achievability ensures that the KPI is realistic given the organisation's resources. Relevance ties the KPI to broader organisational goals, and being time-bound establishes a timeline for achieving the targets.

When constructed thoughtfully, KPIs can illuminate the path to a more sustainable future. They become the benchmarks against which progress is measured, acting as both a yardstick and a motivator. By keeping the focus on key areas, KPIs help allocate resources more efficiently, drive strategic alignment, and facilitate transparent communication with stakeholders.

Inspiration can often be found in the simplicity of well-defined KPIs. Consider the case of Unilever, a company that set an ambitious target to halve the environmental footprint of its products. By breaking this goal down into granular KPIs, they were able to methodically address issues like CO_2 emissions, water usage, and waste in a focused manner. This not only advanced their sustainability agenda but also enhanced their brand value and consumer trust.

Despite their simplicity, well-crafted KPIs have a profound impact. A well-defined KPI acts like a lighthouse, guiding a company through the fog of operational complexities towards clear, strategic objectives. Moreover, they foster a culture of accountability. When everyone from the boardroom to the break room understands the benchmarks for success, achieving sustainability becomes a collective endeavour.

As we move further into an era where sustainability is non-negotiable, the role of KPIs will continue to expand. They will increasingly serve as bridges between different facets of an organisation, from supply chain management to marketing, ensuring that sustainability is not siloed but integrated into the very fabric of business.

Yet, it's essential to remember that KPIs are not static. As market dynamics shift and new sustainability challenges emerge, KPIs should be revisited and recalibrated. This ongoing refinement ensures that the metrics remain relevant and continue to inspire progress. It's a dynamic process, one that underscores the iterative nature of the journey toward sustainability.

Ultimately, defining KPIs is an exercise in both introspection and forward-thinking. It requires organisations to reflect honestly on their current state while keeping an eye on the horizon. Integrating sustainability into the DNA of your business through clearly defined KPIs isn't just about meeting regulatory requirements or societal expectations—it's about ensuring long-term viability and resilience. In this light, KPIs aren't merely indicators—they are instruments of transformation.

Reporting Standards and Frameworks

In our journey towards sustainable transformation, one can't overlook the importance of having robust reporting standards and frameworks. These tools are not mere bureaucratic necessities; they're vital for measuring and communicating the impact of our sustainability efforts. Without a structured approach to reporting, businesses risk flying blind, unable to truly gauge their progress or areas that need improvement.

Every professional, even those with a foundational understanding of finance, recognises that metrics inform strategy. When it comes to sustainability, metrics do more than just inform—they catalyse action. International frameworks like the Global Reporting Initiative (GRI), the Sustainability Accounting Standards Board (SASB), and the Task Force on Climate-related Financial Disclosures (TCFD) offer structured ways to report on diverse sustainability metrics. These frameworks provide a common language that can be understood universally, fostering transparency and accountability.

Imagine a company navigating through a dense forest. Reporting standards are akin to a reliable map that guides them, ensuring they stick to the path toward a sustainable future. The GRI, for example, offers guidelines that encompass a broad range of environmental, social, and governance (ESG) aspects. It's like having a detailed guidebook that ensures no stone is left unturned in the sustainability journey.

SASB, on the other hand, hones in on the financial materiality of sustainability factors. For companies and investors alike, this is game-changing. It bridges the gap between sustainability and tangible financial performance, offering industry-specific standards that ensure relevancy. This isn't just about ticking boxes; it's about gaining insights that drive strategic decisions and operational efficiencies.

Then we have the TCFD, focusing on the financial implications of climate-related risks and opportunities. As climate change becomes an ever-pressing concern, understanding how it impacts business is crucial. The TCFD's recommendations help companies align their strategies with a future that's increasingly shaped by climate realities. It's a call to action—encouraging businesses to be forward-thinking and resilient.

Adopting these reporting frameworks isn't just about compliance; it's about leadership. Companies that commit to rigorous sustainability reporting demonstrate a proactive stance. They send a message to their stakeholders that they are not just participants in the market but leaders in a movement toward a more sustainable world. This builds trust, attracts investment, and boosts reputational capital.

In sum, the right reporting standards and frameworks don't just measure progress—they inspire it. They transform data into actionable insights and foster a culture of accountability and continuous improvement. For mid-career professionals entrenched in the finance and investing world, embracing these tools can revolutionise how you and your organisations approach sustainability. It's a pathway to not just doing well but doing good, driving a meaningful shift towards a resilient and prosperous future.

Chapter 6:
Driving Innovation Through
Sustainability

Innovation has always been the lifeblood of progress, but in today's climate, its very definition is evolving. While traditionally linked to technological advancement and market disruption, innovation is now increasingly intertwined with sustainability. This shift isn't merely a trend; it's a necessary evolution for businesses to remain viable and competitive in an eco-centric marketplace. Companies are realising that sustainability and innovation are not mutually exclusive but can, and should, drive each other.

Green technology is at the forefront of this dynamic change. From renewable energy sources to energy-efficient manufacturing processes, the drive towards sustainability is leading to breakthroughs that were unimaginable a decade ago. Take electric vehicles, for instance. They are no longer niche products but are paving the way for a significant transformation in the transportation sector. Similarly, sustainable agriculture, driven by tech-enabled precision farming, not only promises higher yields but does so while reducing environmental footprints. These examples represent a broader trend where the convergence of sustainability and innovation opens up new investment opportunities, drives competitiveness, and redefines industries.

Research and Development (R&D) is critical for discovering and implementing sustainable solutions. Businesses that prioritise sustainable R&D not only contribute to environmental conservation but also enhance their market position. Companies are increasingly allocating resources to develop biodegradable materials, reduce waste, and create more efficient production techniques. This often involves revisiting and reconstructing their entire supply chains to identify areas for improvement. The commitment to sustainable R&D can turn initial costs into long-term gains by capturing new markets and complying with impending regulations at a fraction of future costs.

Moreover, collaborative innovation is gaining traction. Corporations, academic institutions, startups, and even competitors are coming together to tackle environmental challenges. Open innovation platforms and public-private partnerships are becoming fertile grounds for sustainable breakthroughs. By pooling expertise and resources, these collaborations accelerate the development and implementation of eco-friendly solutions. For example, various conglomerates are working with local governments to develop smart city initiatives that aim for the optimal use of resources while enhancing the quality of urban life.

Ultimately, driving innovation through sustainability requires a paradigm shift in thinking. Old business models that prioritise short-term gains are being dismantled in favour of strategies that consider long-term impacts. Leaders must champion a culture of sustainability that permeates every level of their organisations. It's about reimagining business as usual, where every decision is made with an eye on future generations. By embedding sustainability into the core of innovation, companies are not just future-proofing their operations but also contributing meaningfully to the health of our planet.

Green Technology and Innovation

Green technology and innovation stand as the beacons guiding us through the complex labyrinth of sustainable transformation. At the intersection of ecological mindfulness and cutting-edge science, we find solutions that promise to reshape our industries, leaving a lighter footprint on the planet. Mid-career professionals find themselves in a unique position, bridging the gap between traditional practices and the visionary ethos of sustainability. But what exactly does it mean to infuse our professional lives with green tech, and how can we be the innovators driving this change?

The landscape of green technology is not monolithic; it's a vibrant tapestry woven from various threads – renewable energy, eco-friendly materials, waste reduction strategies, and smart systems harnessing the power of AI and IoT. Each innovation, each breakthrough, is a testament to human ingenuity channelled towards the betterment of our world. Yet, the journey towards adopting these technologies is laden with both opportunities and challenges. For professionals, it's about recognising these potentials and aligning them with corporate goals, making a compelling case both ethically and economically.

It's vital to remember that innovation doesn't happen in a vacuum. It thrives in environments that embrace creativity while being rooted in practical applications. As researchers and developers forge new paths, collaboration becomes crucial. Cross-disciplinary partnerships often yield the most groundbreaking solutions. Engineers, financiers, policy-makers, and end-users must come together, forming ecosystems where sustainable ideas can germinate and flourish. Your role here is not passive; instead, it's about fostering these connections and ensuring that your organisation doesn't just keep up with but leads the drive towards sustainability.

Another critical element lies in understanding the consumer. Today's market is increasingly driven by conscious buyers who value eco-friendly products and services. Green technology isn't just a tick-box exercise; it is central to capturing market share and building brand loyalty. Innovative solutions should meet this demand without compromising on performance or affordability. This dual focus on ecological impact and consumer satisfaction is no longer optional; it's a defining feature of modern business strategy.

In conclusion, green technology and innovation are more than mere buzzwords; they are the linchpins of a sustainable future. As mid-career professionals, you have the vantage point to observe, influence, and implement these technologies within your spheres of influence. By harnessing the power of innovation, you can drive your organisations towards a future where profitability and sustainability are not mutually exclusive but are integrated harmoniously. And in doing so, you'll be contributing to a legacy of progress that respects and preserves the delicate balance of our planet.

R&D for Sustainable Solutions

Innovation needs a heart, a pulse directed by the needs of our planet and its people. Sustainable solutions aren't birthed in isolation. They're conceived through rigorous research and development (R&D), grounded in both scientific inquiry and a profound necessity for change. This isn't just about the next big tech invention but about creating a foundation for future generations to stand on.

The industry landscape is ever-evolving. To stay ahead while remaining grounded in sustainable principles, companies must channel resources into R&D. This means committing to projects with uncertain financial returns yet undeniable environmental dividends. It's a high-stakes game but one worth playing.

Consider the principles of a circular economy where waste essentially becomes non-existent. Innovative R&D efforts in materials science have led to the creation of biodegradable plastics and renewable energy sources, interrupting the traditional, linear cycle of production and disposal. These breakthroughs didn't sprout overnight but were the fruits of relentless experimentation and an unwavering commitment to a better world.

R&D also transcends mere product development. It permeates corporate cultures, pushing firms to rethink their processes, reduce emissions, and minimise waste. Imagine a world where factories break free from pollution constraints by utilising closed-loop systems. This vision isn't utopian; it's already in progress through pioneering R&D initiatives.

It's crucial to understand that sustainable R&D isn't just environmentally focused but also deeply socio-economic. Groundbreaking advancements in technology can render energy more affordable and accessible, enhancing quality of life across various demographics. The ripple effect of such innovations can uplift entire communities.

Nevertheless, pioneering sustainable solutions through R&D can't be relegated to a single department. It has to be a company-wide ethos supported by top-down leadership. The intersection of various disciplines—be it economics, environmental sciences, or social innovation—forms a cohesive strategy that ensures projects align with broader sustainability goals.

Let's not underestimate the power of collaboration in this sphere. Alliances between corporations, academic institutions, and governmental bodies create a fertile ground for cutting-edge R&D. Pooling resources accelerates discovery and implementation, allowing us to scale sustainable solutions at a globally impactful pace.

When you pour your energy into meaningful R&D for sustainable solutions, you're contributing to a legacy extending far beyond profit margins. You're sculpting the framework within which future generations will operate. The goal isn't merely to innovate but to innovate responsibly, recognizing that each breakthrough brings us closer to a sustainable transformation.

Chapter 7:
Risk Management in a Sustainable Context

As we transition towards an eco-economy, it's crucial to acknowledge the risks that come with it. Operating in an ever-changing global landscape necessitates a robust risk management strategy. In this chapter, we'll delve into how businesses can manage risks while keeping sustainability at the forefront.

First, let's reconsider what we traditionally understand as risk. Conventional risk management typically revolves around financial, operational, and market risks. However, in a sustainable context, risks span beyond these dimensions. Environmental, social, and governance (ESG) risks are integral and need to be added to the equation.

Identifying risks in this expanded landscape isn't as straightforward as it was before. For instance, climate change introduces physical risks such as natural disasters, which can disrupt supply chains and operations. Regulatory risks also loom large as governments across the world tighten their environmental policies. Social risks, encompassing public perception and societal impact, have also gained prominence.

Mitigating these risks demands a proactive approach. It's no longer sufficient to react to problems as they arise. Businesses must anticipate potential challenges and implement sustainable practices that build resilience. This might involve investing in renewable energy, adopting circular economy principles, or ensuring ethical labour practices.

One effective way to address these risks is to embed sustainability into your company's risk management framework. Start by conducting comprehensive ESG risk assessments. These assessments should identify potential threats and evaluate their likelihood and impact. From there, develop strategies to mitigate these risks, such as diversifying supply chains or enhancing transparency in reporting.

Building resilience isn't solely about preparing for the worst. It's also about embracing opportunities. For example, companies that prioritise sustainability often discover innovative solutions that can give them a competitive edge. Sustainable practices can lead to cost savings, improved efficiencies, and stronger brand loyalty.

Resilience in business operations requires an adaptive mindset. External conditions can change rapidly, and a rigid approach to risk can be detrimental. Companies should foster a culture of flexibility and continuous improvement. This means regular reviews of risk management strategies and an openness to change.

Incorporating sustainability into risk management is not just a moral necessity; it's becoming an economic imperative. Investors are increasingly scrutinising ESG criteria before committing capital. Failing to align with these criteria can result in a loss of trust and, subsequently, financial support.

In essence, the goal is to integrate sustainability so deeply into the fabric of your business that risk management and sustainable practices become indistinguishable. This integration not only protects your business against potential threats but also positions it to thrive in a future where sustainability is paramount.

As we move forward, remember that every risk is also an opportunity. By managing risks within a sustainable context, businesses can navigate uncertainties while contributing positively to the world around them. This is the essence of modern risk management: it's about securing the future, not just for the company, but for society at large.

Identifying and Mitigating Risks

In the tapestry of economic endeavours, risk isn't just a thread—it's the fabric that binds strategy to reality. When we veer towards sustainable transformations, the importance of identifying and mitigating risks grows exponentially. Risks are ever-present, but understanding their nuances in the context of sustainability adds a layer of complexity, one that demands our full attention and a deft hand at the wheel.

Let's start by acknowledging that risks in sustainable investments are multifaceted. From financial uncertainty to environmental vulnerabilities, there's a kaleidoscope of risks that each firm must untangle. The journey towards sustainability can't be a blind leap; it requires clear vision, precise planning, and impeccable execution. Recognising the potential pitfalls early on helps in crafting resilient strategies that can withstand turbulent tides.

Consider financial risks first. Sustainable projects often require significant capital upfront, with returns that may take longer to materialise. Traditional financial assessments might not capture the long-term benefits or intangible assets that a sustainable initiative adds. Hence, financial modelling must evolve. Incorporating environmental, social, and governance (ESG) factors into these assessments is not just prudent; it's imperative. It means shifting the lens through which we view financial viability and acknowledging the broader spectrum of value.

The unpredictability of regulatory landscapes adds another layer of risk. Governments and regulatory bodies are in a constant state of flux, amending policies and introducing new regulations to address emerging environmental and social issues. Businesses must stay agile, continuously updating their compliance strategies. Ignorance or oversight here can lead to hefty fines, operational disruptions, or, worse, a damaged reputation.

Then there are operational risks, intimately tied to the tangibles—like the raw materials sourced and the technologies implemented. Sourcing sustainable materials often means navigating uncharted territories with fewer suppliers and higher costs. However, the end goal—a resilient and adaptable supply chain—offers a win that far outweighs these initial hurdles. The mission is clear: turn potential weaknesses into strength by investing in long-term, sustainable relationships with suppliers who share your vision.

Climate risks remain ever-looming, amplifying the urgency of our actions. From rising sea levels to catastrophic weather events, climate impacts can disrupt entire industries. Risk assessments must incorporate climate models and forecasts, planning for worst-case scenarios while striving for best-case outcomes. Business continuity plans must be robust, integrating environmental risks into their core frameworks.

Market risks, too, can't be ignored. Consumers are growing more conscious, demanding transparency and accountability from businesses. The risk lies in failing to meet these evolving expectations, leading to a loss of market share. Companies must, therefore, constantly engage with their consumers, understanding their concerns, and aligning their business models to meet these new demands. Robust market research and continuous dialogue with stakeholders become non-negotiable.

Technological risks are another critical consideration. As companies invest in green technologies and innovations, there's always the inherent risk of obsolescence or implementation failures. To mitigate this, businesses need to invest in research and development, ensuring they stay ahead of the curve. Collaborations with tech firms, startups, and academia can provide the edge required to navigate these waters successfully.

One often overlooked but increasingly crucial risk is reputational risk. Today, transparency isn't just expected; it's demanded. Missteps in sustainability can lead to a swift backlash from the public, investors, and regulators. Building a culture of accountability and ethical conduct within the organisation is paramount. Internal audits, transparent reporting, and proactive communication can mitigate reputational damage before it escalates.

Of course, leadership plays a critical role in risk management. It starts from the top, with leaders who not only understand the importance of sustainability but are also committed to integrating risk management into every strategic decision. These leaders foster a culture of vigilance, encouraging employees at all levels to identify and address risks promptly.

No discussion on risk management would be complete without acknowledging the human factor. A well-trained and engaged workforce is an organisation's first line of defence against risk. Investing in education and training programs that focus on sustainability and risk awareness empowers employees to identify risks early and develop innovative solutions. It's a simple truth: people are the bedrock of any risk management strategy.

Collaboration across sectors also offers pathways to mitigate risks. Businesses don't operate in isolation; they're part of a larger ecosystem. Engaging with industry peers, governmental bodies, and non-profit organisations can provide insights and shared strategies for risk mitigation. Collective action often unveils solutions that individual entities might overlook.

Lastly, continuous improvement is the backbone of effective risk management. It's not a 'set and forget' strategy. Regularly reviewing and updating risk management plans ensures that a business remains resilient in the face of new challenges. It's about creating a dynamic, adaptable approach that evolves with changing circumstances.

In the realm of sustainable transformation, identifying and mitigating risks is more than a necessity; it's an opportunity. Each risk unveiled and addressed strengthens the foundations of a sustainable future. It's a challenging path, yes, but one filled with promise for those willing to navigate its complexities with wisdom and resolve.

Building Resilience in Business Operations

Resilience isn't simply about survival; it's about adapting and thriving in the face of adversity. For businesses, the concept of resilience is paramount, more so when the stakes involve sustainable transformation. In the evolving landscape where sustainability is no longer an option but a necessity, embedding resilience in business operations sets the foundation for long-term success and competitiveness.

Imagine resilience as a tree deeply rooted in fertile soil. The roots represent the underlying principles and practices that anchor a business during turbulent times. The branches, reaching skyward, illustrate growth and adaptability, responding to new challenges and seizing emerging opportunities. This analogy is particularly resonant for companies navigating the dual demands of profitability and sustainability.

Let's start with a narrative that's both inspiring and instructive. During the early 2000s, a global electronics company, once an industry leader, faced mounting challenges. Competition was fierce, and environmental regulations grew stricter. The firm pivoted, embedding sustainability into its core strategy. It wasn't just about tweaking processes; it was a holistic re-engineering of their operations. The company invested heavily in green technology, revamped its supply chain, and trained its workforce in sustainable practices. What emerged was a more resilient, innovative, and ultimately profitable enterprise. This transformation wasn't instantaneous, but it underscored a critical principle: resilience is built through intention and sustained effort.

The essence of building resilience lies in understanding and preparing for risks, not just reacting to them. It starts with a robust risk management framework that identifies potential pitfalls in both traditional and sustainability-focused domains. Climate change, regulatory shifts, and evolving consumer preferences are just a few variables that can impact business operations. A resilient company doesn't merely anticipate these risks; it actively mitigates them through strategic planning and adaptive measures.

Consider the versatility of diverse revenue streams. When businesses rely heavily on a single product or market, they expose themselves to greater risk. Diversifying products, services, and markets can cushion against unforeseen disruptions. This approach serves a dual purpose in a sustainability context: it opens new avenues for eco-friendly innovations and reduces dependency on unsustainable revenue sources.

Operational efficiency is another cornerstone of resilience. Efficient use of resources—be it energy, materials, or human capital— not only cuts costs but also enhances a company's ability to cope with external shocks. Implementing circular economy principles, such as recycling and resource optimisation, can significantly boost resilience. Imagine a manufacturing firm that reuses waste materials in its production process; it reduces waste disposal costs, conserves raw materials, and insulates itself from volatile market prices.

The agility to innovate is crucial. In an age where technological advancements are swift and customer expectations evolve rapidly, businesses must stay ahead of the curve. This demands a culture of perpetual innovation, where sustainability is a key driver. Research and development (R&D) investments dedicated to green technologies not only address environmental concerns but also place companies at the forefront of market trends.

Resilience also stems from robust stakeholder relationships. Open communication channels with suppliers, customers, employees, and the wider community build a network of trust and cooperation. When a crisis hits, these relationships can provide critical support. For example, during a supply chain disruption, strong supplier relationships can facilitate quicker recovery times and alternative sourcing solutions.

The quest for resilience is incomplete without considering the welfare of the workforce. Employees are the heartbeat of any organisation, and their well-being directly influences operational integrity and morale. Providing a safe, inclusive, and supportive work environment fosters employee loyalty and productivity. Programs that encourage work-life balance, continuous learning, and personal growth contribute to a resilient workforce poised to tackle challenges head-on.

As sustainability takes centre stage, compliance with environmental regulations becomes non-negotiable. But resilience transcends mere compliance; it involves proactive engagement with regulatory changes and industry standards. Companies that anticipate regulatory trends and align their operations accordingly can avoid costly penalties and gain a competitive edge. This proactive stance also signals to stakeholders that the company is committed to sustainable and ethical practices.

Financial resilience deserves special attention. Traditional financial metrics alone can no longer gauge a company's long-term viability in a sustainability-driven market. Integrating Environmental, Social, and Governance (ESG) factors into financial assessments provides a more holistic view of risks and opportunities. Access to green finance, sustainability bonds, and other innovative financial instruments can offer the necessary capital to support resilient and sustainable operations.

Strategic partnerships play a pivotal role in bolstering resilience. Collaborating with other businesses, NGOs, and government entities can amplify efforts and share risks. Partnerships allow companies to leverage external expertise, technologies, and resources that may be beyond their immediate reach. For instance, joint ventures in renewable energy projects can mitigate individual risk and enhance collective benefits.

Transparency and accountability form the bedrock of trust. Regularly communicating progress on sustainability goals, operational challenges, and risk management strategies builds credibility. Transparent reporting not only meets regulatory demands but resonates with stakeholders, including investors who increasingly prioritise ESG criteria.

Looking forward, building resilience in business operations is a continuous journey, not a destination. It's about creating a sustainable, adaptable, and thriving enterprise. Each decision and strategy must be viewed through the lens of resilience, ensuring the organisation is well-equipped to navigate the uncertainties and demands of a rapidly changing world. The ultimate aim is not just to survive but to flourish and lead by example in the pursuit of a sustainable future.

As we navigate this complex landscape, remember that the seeds of resilience, once sown with intention and nurtured with consistent effort, can yield a robust and sustainable business that stands the test of time. The journey towards resilience requires vision, commitment, and an unwavering belief in the power of sustainable transformation.

Chapter 8:
The Role of Policy and Regulation

In our journey toward sustainable transformation, policy and regulation serve not just as guardrails, but as powerful accelerators. Policies set the course, while regulations ensure we remain on track, compelling even the most reluctant to follow suit. This isn't about restrictive boundaries; rather, it involves setting the framework within which businesses can innovate and thrive sustainably. They carve out the rules of engagement, fostering a predictable environment where long-term strategies can flourish.

Governments worldwide have employed an array of regulatory tools to boost sustainable initiatives. From carbon pricing mechanisms to green certifications, these instruments shift behaviours and re-align economic incentives with ecological goals. Regulatory frameworks hold the potential to turn environmental responsibility into economic opportunity. For instance, stringent emissions standards have driven automakers to innovate in electric and hybrid vehicle technologies, turning a compliance obligation into a market differentiator.

Engagement with policymakers is not a passive endeavour. Businesses must actively participate in the regulatory process to ensure that policies not only safeguard the environment but also consider the economic realities of industries. Collaboration between the public and private sectors can produce balanced regulations that drive sustainability without stifling competitiveness. This proactive stance allows business leaders to shape policies that encourage sustainable growth, rather than merely reacting to imposed mandates.

Regulatory landscapes are by nature dynamic, continuously evolving in response to scientific insights, societal expectations, and economic conditions. Staying ahead requires vigilance and adaptability. Enterprises should not perceive regulatory compliance as a mere cost of doing business, but as a strategic component of their growth strategy. By anticipating changes and aligning their operations accordingly, companies can mitigate risks and seize early mover advantages in emerging sustainable markets.

Ultimately, the role of policy and regulation extends beyond enforcement; it fosters a culture of sustainability. By setting ambitious yet achievable targets, regulations can inspire innovation and drive the collective shift towards a more sustainable future. Business leaders, policymakers, and society must work in concert to ensure these frameworks are robust, fair, and forward-thinking, laying the groundwork for a thriving, sustainable economy that benefits all.

Understanding Relevant Regulations

When discussing the landscape of sustainability, it's impossible to ignore the vital role that regulations play. At first glance, regulations might seem like a set of limitations, a series of hurdles to jump over. However, these guidelines are far more than bureaucratic red tape; they're the bedrock of sustainable transformations, helping align corporate actions with broader environmental and social goals.

Various regulations at local, national, and international levels strive to usher businesses towards sustainability. Whether it's greenhouse gas emissions guidelines, water usage restrictions, or compliance with international sustainability standards, these rules form the framework within which businesses can operate responsibly. Engaging with, understanding, and integrating these regulations into corporate strategy is not just a necessity but a stepping stone towards innovation and long-term success.

To truly grasp the importance of these regulations, consider their underlying purpose: to create a world where economic growth doesn't come at the expense of the planet or society. The regulations are founded on years of research, dialogue among experts, and negotiations among stakeholders, reflecting a collective desire for a more balanced and equitable world. They are, in essence, the manifestation of our societal commitment to sustainable development.

While navigating the regulatory landscape might seem daunting, it offers unprecedented opportunities for businesses willing to take the leap. Take, for instance, the European Union's Green Deal, which paves the way for innovation in energy efficiency and renewable resources. Staying ahead of regulatory changes often means accessing new markets, gaining consumer trust, and securing financial incentives designed to support sustainable initiatives. In this sense, regulations can become catalysts for growth.

Moreover, the intricacy of regulations necessitates a proactive approach. Companies that maintain compliance rather than exceed it may find themselves at a competitive disadvantage. The ever-evolving regulatory environment demands agility, foresight, and a steadfast commitment to sustainability. Those that anticipate regulatory shifts can adapt more easily and often reshape the market in their favour. Compliance, therefore, should be viewed as a baseline, not the pinnacle, of corporate sustainability strategy.

For mid-career professionals aiming to spearhead sustainable initiatives, understanding relevant regulations goes beyond mere awareness. It's about embedding this understanding into your organisational culture, fostering a regulatory mindset that permeates all levels of operation. Seek clarity on how each regulation impacts various aspects of your business, from supply chain logistics to consumer-facing operations, and maintain an open dialogue with policymakers and industry bodies.

In conclusion, recognising and internalising relevant regulations is a powerful motivator for transforming the way we do business. They guide us to take responsibility, innovate, and ultimately, thrive within a system committed to sustainability. As we delve deeper into engaging with policymakers in the next section, remember that each regulation is not just an obligation but an opportunity: to drive positive change, secure a competitive edge, and contribute to a sustainable future.

Engaging with Policymakers

Transforming industries towards sustainable futures isn't just an internal corporate affair; it's inherently linked with the broader frameworks constructed by policymakers. These policymakers set the stage upon which companies operate, innovate, and evolve. Engaging effectively with them is akin to harmonising a symphony, where every instrument has its critical moment, and timing is everything.

Your journey in sustainable transformation must include a clear understanding of the regulatory landscape. This isn't merely a box to tick off but an ongoing dialogue. Engage with policymakers not out of obligation, but because these interactions can profoundly shape the direction and impact of your sustainability initiatives. Imagine sitting at a table where the future of business regulations is penned – your insights can contribute to crafting regulations that bolster not only your enterprise but the entire industry.

Policymakers often balance competing interests and make decisions on issues where the stakes are enormously high. Think of the European Union's Green Deal or carbon pricing mechanisms. These aren't trivial matters but grand designs to reshape economies. To effectively engage, it's essential to speak their language. Offer comprehensive data, impactful case studies, and articulate the long-term benefits your sustainable practices bring, not just to your business but to the wider society.

Approaching policymakers should be strategic and purpose-driven. Form alliances with other businesses, non-profits, and academic institutions to present a united front. There's undeniable power in numbers. Collective lobbying for incentivising renewable energy or implementing circular economy principles can resonate more profoundly than solitary voices. Remember, it's about demonstrating that sustainable policies are not merely regulatory impositions but opportunities for economic growth and societal betterment.

Effective engagement is a marathon, not a sprint. It requires persistence, patience, and preparedness. Initiate the dialogue with detailed white papers, join industry forums, and participate in advisory committees. This isn't about ticking off a checklist but fostering a meaningful partnership. Policymakers often need insights and feedback from those on the frontlines of industry to create practical and impactful regulations. Your role can be instrumental in shaping policies that are not only feasible but enable businesses to thrive sustainably.

Consider the role of storytelling when engaging with policymakers. Narratives that highlight the tangible benefits of your sustainable efforts can be compelling. Discuss how your waste reduction initiatives have led to tangible cost savings, or how investing in renewable energy has enhanced your brand's reputation. These stories make the abstract real and underscore the human element behind policy decisions. They illuminate the path forward while making the case for urgency.

Engaging with policymakers also requires an understanding of the political and social climates. Regulatory landscapes are not static; they evolve with the changing priorities of society. Engage not just with policymakers but with the communities they serve. Attend public consultations, contribute to think tanks, and stay abreast of the evolving dialogues around sustainability. Through this, your engagement will be not only more informed but also more impactful.

Transparency and integrity in your communications are paramount. Be clear about your objectives and the mutual benefits. Policymakers appreciate honesty and clear intentions. By presenting your company's achievements and challenges candidly, you build trust and create a foundation for long-term partnerships.

Finally, consider the ripple effects of your engagement. Well-crafted policies can lead to a cascade of benefits, from enhanced investor confidence and consumer loyalty to a healthier, more sustainable environment. By engaging actively and conscientiously with policymakers, you're not just advocating for your company or industry, but for a future where sustainable practices become the norm, not the exception.

In essence, treating engagement with policymakers as a core component of your sustainable strategy rather than an add-on ensures a robust, forward-facing approach. It's about aligning your business's journey with the legislative roadmap, ensuring both entities move in tandem towards a common goal – a more sustainable, prosperous future for all.

Chapter 9:
Stakeholder Engagement and Communication

Understanding the fabric of stakeholder engagement and effective communication is crucial in driving sustainable transformation. In the complex web of today's business environments, where stakeholders range from investors and employees to communities and regulators, communication isn't just about conveying information; it's about building genuine relationships founded on trust and mutual respect. Imagine a world where businesses didn't just inform but inspired, where every conversation became a catalyst for sustainable change. This vision isn't far-fetched when one recognises the power of stakeholder engagement as a tool for transformative action.

To navigate this intricate landscape, identifying key stakeholders and tailoring communication strategies to their unique perspectives is essential. Who are the individuals and groups that influence or are influenced by your company's sustainability endeavours? Think beyond the obvious - shareholders and customers - and consider local communities, NGOs, and even future generations. The essence of impactful, sustainable transformation lies in creating channels of dialogue and collaboration that cut across these diverse groups. This means crafting messages that resonate on a personal level, addressing concerns with empathy, and listening - truly listening - to feedback.

Effective communication strategies aren't just about the right words; they're about the right actions. Transparency and accountability are the cornerstones. Share your triumphs, yes, but don't shy away from discussing your struggles and the lessons learned. People are more likely to invest their time, energy, and resources in businesses that present an authentic narrative. Communication must evolve into a continuous, iterative process, where actions reinforce words and stakeholders feel genuinely part of the journey towards sustainability. In this dance of engagement, let each step be a testament to your commitment to a sustainable future.

Identifying Key Stakeholders

In the journey towards sustainable transformation, one must first begin by identifying the key stakeholders involved. This isn't merely an exercise in listing names; it is a profound exploration of relationships, roles, and the intricate web of influence. Every stakeholder carries a unique perspective and set of interests that can significantly impact the trajectory of sustainability efforts.

Stakeholders can be broadly classified into internal and external groups. Internal stakeholders are those within the organisation, like employees, management, and shareholders. External stakeholders encompass a wider array, including customers, suppliers, community groups, regulators, and even competitors. Recognising who these individuals and groups are is paramount to crafting effective engagement and communication strategies.

The importance of involving employees can't be overstated. They are the heartbeat of any organisation, driving daily operations and embodying the company's values. Engaging them in sustainability efforts requires an understanding of their motivations and concerns. Transparent communication and active participation can foster a sense of ownership and commitment to sustainable goals.

Management and leadership play a crucial role as well. Their buy-in and advocacy are essential for embedding sustainability into the corporate strategy. They can mobilise resources, influence organisational culture, and set the tone for company-wide initiatives. Identifying key leaders who can champion sustainability efforts can create a ripple effect throughout the business.

Shareholders, particularly in publicly traded companies, have a vested interest in the organisation's financial performance. However, there's a growing recognition that long-term profitability and sustainability are not mutually exclusive. Engaging with shareholders about how sustainable practices can enhance value and ensure future resilience can secure their support.

Customers and clients are another pivotal group. Consumers today are more informed and conscientious about the social and environmental impact of their purchases. Identifying and understanding the expectations and values of this group can guide product development and marketing strategies that resonate with sustainable principles.

Suppliers and business partners form the backbone of the supply chain. Their practices and policies have direct implications on an organisation's sustainability credentials. Engaging with these stakeholders involves assessing their commitment to sustainability, setting shared goals, and fostering collaboration towards common objectives.

The community in which a business operates holds significant stakes in its activities. Local communities are affected by environmental practices, employment policies, and corporate social responsibility initiatives. Building strong relationships with community leaders and organisations can enhance mutual trust and support. This, in turn, can lead to a more favourable operating environment and a positive corporate image.

Regulators and policymakers shape the framework within which businesses operate. Understanding the regulatory landscape and actively engaging with these stakeholders ensures compliance and can influence the development of more conducive policies. Advocacy and participation in policy dialogues can help shape regulations that balance economic, social, and environmental goals.

Another often-overlooked group comprises the competitors. While it may seem counterintuitive, collaborating with competitors on sustainability issues can lead to industry-wide improvements and innovations. Identifying shared challenges and working together can drive collective progress that benefits all parties involved.

Media and opinion leaders also wield substantial influence. They can amplify messages, shape public perception, and hold organisations accountable. Engaging with this group requires careful messaging and transparency to foster positive coverage and build a constructive dialogue around sustainability efforts.

Academia and research institutions can provide valuable insights and innovations. Partnering with these stakeholders can enhance knowledge sharing, drive research and development, and lead to the implementation of cutting-edge solutions. Identifying key academic figures and institutions aligned with your sustainability goals can open doors to valuable collaborations.

Non-governmental organisations (NGOs) and civil society organisations often act as watchdogs and advocates for social and environmental causes. Engaging with NGOs can provide critical insights, foster partnerships, and enhance an organisation's credibility. Identifying relevant NGOs and understanding their interests can lead to mutually beneficial collaborations.

Investors, particularly those focused on responsible investing, are increasingly influential in promoting sustainability. Identifying these stakeholders and communicating how sustainable practices align with financial returns can attract investment and drive sustainable growth. This also includes understanding the specific criteria and frameworks investors use to evaluate sustainability.

Finally, understanding the interconnectedness of these stakeholder groups is crucial. Actions and decisions in one area can ripple through and impact others. A holistic approach to identifying and engaging stakeholders can create a more resilient and responsive strategy for sustainability transformation.

The process of identifying key stakeholders is continuous and dynamic. It involves regular re-evaluation and adaptation to ensure all relevant voices are heard and all interests considered. This lays the foundation for meaningful engagement and effective communication, ultimately driving the sustainable transformation forward.

Effective Communication Strategies

When we delve into the intricate dance of sustainability, effective communication with stakeholders stands as a pillar. It's not merely about disseminating information; it's about crafting a narrative that invites action and understanding. Imagine for a moment, a diverse set of individuals with varied interests and perspectives. Our mission is to weave a coherent story that resonates across this mosaic.

First, we must recognise the language of clarity. Speaking in ambiguous terms or complex jargon alienates rather than engages. Use simple and direct terms, ensuring your message cuts through the noise. It isn't a dilution of complexity, but a distillation of essence. When addressing financial nuances of sustainability, avoid financialese. Instead, frame it in the context of impact and long-term benefit, which is a language every stakeholder understands.

Secondly, timing matters. Communication is not a one-off event but a continual dialogue that progresses and evolves. Stakeholders need updates, not just milestones. Regular, bite-sized pieces of information help maintain interest and engagement, fostering a sense of inclusion in the journey. Consider a quarterly update that's more conversational than formal, designed to spark curiosity and invite questions.

Empathy is a powerful tool. It requires us to step into the shoes of our stakeholders, understand their fears, aspirations, and motivations. When we communicate from a place of empathy, we acknowledge their stakes and perspectives. This fosters trust and opens the door to a more genuine connection. Instead of just presenting charts, share stories of real people affected by sustainability initiatives. Make it personal, relatable.

Visuals cannot be underestimated. Human brains process visuals faster than text, and in many cases, more effectively. Infographics, charts, and videos offer a dynamic way to convey complex information. For instance, a well-crafted video demonstrating the lifecycle of a sustainable product can be far more engaging than a written report.

The use of narrative creates emotional resonance. Human beings are wired for stories, and a compelling narrative can bridge the gap between facts and emotions. When you narrate the journey of a company transitioning to sustainable practices, include the struggles, the breakthroughs, and the human spirit that drives change. This connection to real-world experiences underscores the tangible benefits of sustainability.

Stakeholder engagement isn't one-size-fits-all. Tailor your approach based on the stakeholder's level of involvement and interest. Investors might appreciate detailed financial analyses, while community members may be more interested in social and environmental impacts. Customising the message ensures that it lands effectively, fulfilling the unique informational needs of each group.

Feedback loops are essential. Communication should be a two-way street. Encourage stakeholders to voice their concerns, provide suggestions, and participate in the conversation. This not only enhances transparency but also helps in refining strategies. Establishing forums, conducting surveys, and holding Q&A sessions can be instrumental in gathering valuable insights.

Transparency builds credibility. Today's stakeholders are well-informed and expect organisations to be forthright with their challenges and setbacks, not just their successes. Providing an honest, balanced view of sustainability efforts—highlighting both achievements and areas for improvement—can bolster stakeholder trust and engagement.

Utilising diverse communication channels broadens your reach. In our digital age, leveraging platforms like social media, webinars, emails, and traditional media can ensure your message reaches a wider audience. Each channel has its strengths, and a multi-channel strategy can cater to varying preferences, maximising impact.

Keep the message consistent. Consistency across all forms of communication builds a strong, recognisable brand narrative around sustainability. Whether it's an annual report, a social media post, or a community event, the core message should align seamlessly, reinforcing the organisation's commitment and vision.

Engaging visuals combined with interactivity can elevate the communication experience. Interactive formats such as workshops, virtual reality tours, and hands-on community projects allow stakeholders to experience sustainability firsthand. This active engagement can turn abstract concepts into concrete realisations.

Humility in communication recognises that no journey to sustainability is without its stumbles. Share lessons learned and how setbacks have informed better strategies. This transparency not only builds trust but also portrays the organisation's resilience and commitment to continuous improvement.

Crafting thoughtful, reflective content that challenges stakeholders to consider their role in sustainable transformation can spark deeper engagement. Pose questions, share thought-provoking content, and invite reflection. This not only educates but also empowers stakeholders to think critically about their contributions.

Finally, leading by example sets the standard. Ensure that internal practices reflect the sustainability messages being communicated. Authenticity begins at home; when stakeholders see that an organisation's actions align with its words, it solidifies credibility and fosters deeper trust.

In the end, effective communication strategies in stakeholder engagement are about more than just information exchange. They are about fostering connections, building trust, and inspiring collective action towards a sustainable future. Let every word, image, and gesture embody this mission.

Chapter 10:
Financing the Sustainable Transformation

We're at a tipping point where sustainability isn't just a buzzword—it's a necessity. Yet, one pivotal question remains: how do we finance this transformation? Traditional financial models focused on short-term gains are increasingly at odds with long-term sustainability goals. Strategies must evolve to bridge this gap, aligning financial incentives with ecological imperatives. This chapter explores how accessing capital for sustainability projects can be both a moral and economic imperative.

Accessing capital for sustainability projects demands a nuanced understanding of emerging financial instruments. Green bonds, social impact bonds, and sustainability-linked loans have become essential cogs in this machine. These tools don't just offer capital; they provide a framework for accountability, measuring success by both financial returns and environmental impact. The shift towards these financial instruments marks a departure from short-sighted gains to creating long-lasting value.

The role of banks and financial institutions is crucial but often misunderstood. These entities are not just gatekeepers of capital; they're partners in the journey towards a sustainable future. By embedding environmental, social, and governance (ESG) criteria into their lending practices, banks can help de-risk investments in sustainable projects. Additionally, public-private partnerships are emerging as powerful vehicles for financing large-scale initiatives. Such collaborations can distribute risk while amplifying impact.

Venture capital and private equity also have significant roles to play. These investors are naturally inclined towards high-risk, high-reward scenarios, making them well-suited to back disruptive sustainable technologies. When aligned with clear sustainability goals, venture capital investments can drive innovation and enable companies to scale rapidly. However, it's crucial for these financial backers to maintain a focus on long-term ecological outcomes, not just monetary returns.

Lastly, individual investors are waking up to their potential impact. Through green investment funds and direct investments in sustainable companies, they can influence the market and encourage corporate responsibility. Crowdfunding platforms for green projects are particularly noteworthy, democratizing the investment landscape. They allow regular people to put their money where their values are, reinforcing that sustainable transformation is both a collective responsibility and opportunity.

Accessing Capital for Sustainability Projects

Accessing capital for sustainability projects isn't just about finding money. It's about aligning financial resources with the vision of a greener, more equitable future. For mid-career professionals with some grounding in finance, understanding how to harness this capital is vital to driving impactful change in their organisations.

First and foremost, traditional investment routes such as bank loans and bonds have evolved to cater to sustainability initiatives. Green bonds, for instance, have emerged as a key instrument. These bonds are specifically earmarked to fund environmental projects and have garnered growing interest in financial markets. What makes them attractive is their dual promise: financial returns and a positive environmental impact.

Understanding the landscape of sustainable finance requires delving into the more specialized instruments designed for eco-friendly initiatives. Beyond green bonds, mechanisms such as sustainability-linked loans tie borrowing costs to the borrower's performance on environmental, social, and governance (ESG) criteria. This not only incentivises companies to meet sustainability targets but also offers a transparent way for investors to track progress.

Venture capital (VC) is also increasingly tuned into the potential of green startups. Investors are on the lookout for companies driving technological innovation in areas like renewable energy, waste management, and climate tech. As a professional, pitching these futuristic endeavours means presenting not just a viable business model but a compelling story of environmental stewardship.

Additionally, crowdfunding platforms have emerged as democratic spaces where public support can fuel sustainability projects. Platforms like Kickstarter and Indiegogo have seen a surge in environmentally-focused campaigns, allowing companies to raise capital directly from engaged communities. This approach doesn't just provide funding; it also builds a loyal customer base or stakeholder network from day one.

Corporations themselves are becoming financiers in this arena. Corporate venture funds are increasingly being directed towards sustainable innovations that align with the parent company's strategic goals. For instance, tech giants and automotive leaders are investing in green technologies that bolster their sustainability credentials and drive future growth.

Government grants and subsidies remain crucial, often acting as the bedrock funding for early-stage or high-risk sustainability projects. These financial aids are designed to mitigate the initial risk and make sustainability projects more attractive to private investors. Navigating these funds requires staying abreast of policy changes and knowing where to look, whether it's international bodies like the World Bank or national agencies dedicated to environmental protection.

One cannot overlook the role of private equity in this context. Private equity funds dedicated to sustainability are growing, seeking out investments that promise not only strong returns but also a measurable impact on environmental outcomes. For mid-career professionals, understanding how to present these opportunities to private equity investors can be a game-changer.

Institutional investors also play a pivotal role, driven by their growing commitment to ESG principles. Pension funds, university endowments, and sovereign wealth funds are increasingly demanding sustainable options. This demand prompts companies to adopt and highlight sustainable practices to attract this significant capital flow.

Philanthropic funding adds another dimension to the financing mix. Foundations and philanthropic organisations are keen to support innovative sustainability projects that align with their missions. This type of funding often comes with fewer strings attached compared to traditional investment, allowing for more experimental approaches that could lead to groundbreaking advancements.

As the landscape of sustainable finance broadens, so too do the strategies for accessing this capital. Blended finance, for example, combines public and private investment to lower risks and enhance returns for sustainability projects. This approach capitalises on the strengths of diverse funding sources to achieve a common goal.

Partnerships and alliances are another strategic avenue. Collaborative efforts can pool resources, share risks, and maximise impact. Engaging with networks such as the Global Impact Investing

Network (GIIN) or the UN Global Compact can open doors to capital and expertise previously out of reach.

Ultimately, the journey to accessing capital for sustainability projects is multifaceted. It requires an integration of traditional and innovative financial mechanisms, a keen understanding of stakeholder needs, and an unwavering commitment to sustainable principles. As you navigate this landscape, remember that every step taken toward secure funding is a step toward a more resilient and sustainable future.

As mid-career professionals, you are in a unique position to bridge the gap between traditional finance and innovative sustainability solutions. Your experience and insights are critical in shaping the funding strategies that will drive tomorrow's green innovations. Embrace this challenge with the knowledge that your efforts are steering us closer to a sustainable transformation.

Role of Banks and Financial Institutions

The transformative power banks and financial institutions wield in promoting sustainability can't be underestimated. To fully grasp their influence, we ought to examine how these entities fund, shape, and sometimes hinder sustainable initiatives. Their pivotal position in our financial ecosystem makes them gatekeepers to the capital essential for a sustainable future.

Let us take a moment to consider the role of finance. Money, in all its forms, isn't just a medium of exchange—it's a potent instrument of change. Banks and financial institutions have budgets that dwarf those of most governments, and they're uniquely positioned to drive the green agenda by funding sustainable projects and innovations. But how does this process unfold in real-world contexts?

Firstly, let's explore their core function: lending. Traditional lending practices often prioritize short-term gains and low-risk ventures. However, banks are increasingly recognising that sustainable projects, despite their initial perceived risks, offer long-term profitability and societal benefits. A growing number of financial institutions are establishing green lending criteria, setting aside specific funds for projects that meet sustainability benchmarks.

Moreover, financing renewable energy is a significant area where banks can make a difference. For example, large-scale solar farms, wind energy projects, and geothermal plants require substantial initial investments. Banks that lead in green financing are not only providing capital but also promoting technology that reduces carbon footprints and fosters environmental responsibility.

Another critical aspect is the issuance of green bonds. These financial instruments are designed to raise funds for projects with environmental benefits. They're growing in popularity, with banks and financial institutions increasingly underwriting them. Green bonds finance everything from clean water projects to energy-efficient buildings, bridging the gap between sustainable ambitions and concrete initiatives.

However, it's not just about doling out money. Portfolio management plays a crucial role. Investment managers now face growing pressure to consider Environmental, Social, and Governance (ESG) factors in their decision-making processes. By doing so, they encourage companies to adopt sustainable practices, knowing that their funding is contingent upon meeting these criteria.

So, what about the banks' governance? Financial institutions are adopting more robust internal policies that align with sustainable values. From setting carbon-neutral goals to incorporating sustainability into their corporate strategies, these entities are slowly but steadily transforming their operational ethos. Standard Chartered, for instance, has committed to aligning its lending portfolio with the Paris Agreement's goals, setting a precedent for others to follow.

It's also important to explore the ripple effects their influence creates. Banks and financial institutions often serve as catalysts, encouraging other sectors to adopt sustainable practices. When a business sees that its access to capital hinges on its sustainability metrics, it receives a compelling incentive to change. This knock-on effect amplifies the impact far beyond the initial investment.

Yet, the journey hasn't been wholly smooth. There are obstacles aplenty—regulatory frameworks lag behind, and there's often a mismatch between short-term financial goals and long-term sustainability aims. For real change to take root, a harmonious alignment between public policy and financial incentives must be nurtured, ensuring that the rules of the game reward sustainable endeavours.

Let's not forget the persuasive power of advocacy either. Many banks and financial institutions engage in policy dialogues, pushing for regulations that promote sustainability. It's a dynamic interaction, where these organisations are both influencers and respondents, shaping and adapting to the emerging regulatory landscape.

Education and training within these institutions are fundamental as well. Equipping staff with the knowledge and tools to evaluate sustainable projects is essential. It transforms the theoretical potential of green finance into actionable strategies. BNP Paribas, for example, has instituted training programmes focused on ESG factors, empowering its employees to make informed, impactful decisions.

Engaging with stakeholders is another avenue where banks excel. They liaise with everyone from small business owners to multinational corporations, building a diverse network dedicated to sustainable transformation. This collaborative approach fosters a culture of shared responsibility, one that reverberates through various sectors and societal layers.

Moreover, digital innovation also holds immense promise. Fintech solutions, blockchain for transparent tracking, and AI for predictive analytics about environmental impact are opening new frontiers. Financial institutions that leverage these technologies can offer more efficient, reliable, and scalable solutions to their clients, thereby reinforcing the sustainability agenda.

Affluent in resources and strategic prowess, banks and financial institutions must continually strive to dismantle barriers to sustainable financing. By creating frameworks that lower the entry thresholds for sustainable projects, they can democratise access to green capital, fostering inclusive economic growth.

It's a complex mosaic, where each action, policy shift, and investment decision weaves into a broader tapestry of sustainable transformation. The task ahead isn't merely to channel funds but to shift paradigms, turning every financial decision into a step toward a greener future. The role of banks and financial institutions extends beyond balance sheets—it's about sculpting a world where profit and planet can coexist harmoniously. They are, undeniably, architects of the sustainable future we all aspire to build.

Chapter 11:
The Impact on Human Capital

Human capital is the lifeblood of any organisation, but its role in sustainable transformation is often underestimated. As we shift towards more eco-conscious business models, the significance of retaining and developing quality jobs becomes undeniable. No longer can companies afford to treat employees as mere cogs in a machine. Each individual, with their unique skills and aspirations, becomes integral to the collective effort.

Retaining quality talent necessitates more than just competitive salaries. It calls for instilling a sense of purpose, aligned with sustainable goals. Workers today crave meaning beyond the paycheck, seeking roles that contribute positively to the environment and society. The correlation here is clear: higher engagement drives productivity and innovation, which are crucial for long-term sustainability. Companies that acknowledge this symbiosis will not only attract but also retain top talent.

The transformation towards a green economy demands new competencies. Traditional skill sets may no longer suffice. Therefore, training and education become imperative. Investing in upskilling and reskilling employees ensures they are not left behind as industries evolve. Green technology, sustainable practices, and innovative thinking should be at the forefront of training programmes. By doing so, organisations build a workforce that's not only adaptable but also leaders in their fields.

Furthermore, a commitment to human capital extends beyond immediate employees. It influences supply chains, partnerships, and even customer bases. Collaboration becomes key. Firms that promote sustainable practices will naturally gravitate towards like-minded partners, creating a ripple effect across industries. This collaborative ecosystem fosters shared learning and rapid advancements in sustainability initiatives.

In closing, the focus on human capital in sustainable transformation is not just a corporate responsibility—it's a strategic necessity. The companies that pioneer in this realm will set a precedent, driving societal change and capturing the economic benefits of a motivated, well-trained workforce. Ultimately, the investment in human capital pays dividends in creating resilient, forward-thinking enterprises ready to navigate the challenges of the future.

Retaining and Developing Quality Jobs

As businesses strive towards sustainable transformation, retaining and developing quality jobs emerges as a pivotal challenge. It's not merely about maintaining current jobs but ensuring they evolve with the needs of a greener economy. The focus transforms from preserving employment in its traditional sense to fostering roles that contribute to and thrive within an eco-economic framework.

The essence of quality jobs lies in their alignment with sustainable practices. Roles that embrace sustainability offer more than just economic benefits; they provide a sense of purpose and fulfilment to employees. Job satisfaction and retention rates improve when employees perceive their work as contributing to a larger, worthwhile cause.

Just as ecological balance is fundamental to our planet, job satisfaction is crucial for the sustenance of any workforce. Employees who find their work environment congruent with their values are more likely to stay and grow within the organization. This realization requires a shift from traditional performance metrics to more holistic ones that consider the well-being and continuous development of the workforce.

Developing quality jobs calls for a commitment to continual learning and adaptation. The green economy is dynamic, bringing with it a myriad of new technologies and processes. Companies must invest in robust training programs that prepare employees for these changes. This investment isn't a sunk cost but one that yields high returns through increased efficiency, innovation, and loyalty.

Equally critical is the role of leadership in inspiring and supporting this development. Leaders who champion sustainability within their organizations set the tone for a culture that values long-term impacts over short-term gains. Through transparent communication and inclusive practices, these leaders can foster a sense of shared purpose.

Moreover, retaining quality jobs involves creating an inclusive environment where diverse perspectives are valued. A workforce that reflects various backgrounds and experiences is better equipped to drive innovation and problem-solving. Diversity becomes an asset, enabling organizations to navigate the complexities of sustainable transformation more effectively.

Career pathways within the green economy must be clear and compelling. Employees should see opportunities for advancement tied to sustainable initiatives. Providing avenues for career growth not only enhances retention but also ensures that the expertise within the organization grows in alignment with its sustainable goals.

Furthermore, companies need to recognize the importance of work-life balance in job satisfaction. Sustainable workplaces are not just environmentally friendly but also human-centric. Policies that support flexible work arrangements, mental health, and overall well-being contribute significantly to employee retention and productivity.

Financial incentives play a role too. Performance-related pay and bonuses linked to sustainable achievements incentivize employees to align their efforts with the company's green goals. When employees see a tangible link between their contributions to sustainability and their financial rewards, their commitment levels naturally rise.

It's crucial to understand that quality jobs go beyond the geographical confines of an office. Remote work, facilitated by advancements in digital technology, has become a key component of modern employment. Building a remote-friendly culture that's both sustainable and inclusive aids in retaining top talent from diverse locations.

Collaborations with educational institutions can also bolster efforts in developing quality jobs. By partnering with universities and vocational schools, companies can help shape curricula that align with future industry needs. Internships and apprenticeship programs can serve as vital pipelines for integrating fresh talent into the workforce.

Additionally, mentorship programs play a pivotal role. Experienced employees can guide newer recruits, sharing insights and fostering a culture of knowledge transfer that's crucial for the sustainability of quality roles within the organization.

Monitoring and feedback mechanisms are essential. Regularly assessing employee satisfaction and professional development can identify areas for improvement. Constructive feedback loops ensure that adjustments can be made promptly, maintaining a workforce that feels valued and heard.

Lastly, celebrating successes, both big and small, reinforces commitment to sustainable goals. Recognizing and rewarding teams and individuals who contribute significantly to these objectives fosters a positive environment. It's in these celebrations that the essence of sustainable transformation is felt most acutely, bolstering the willingness to continue the journey.

In conclusion, retaining and developing quality jobs within the realm of human capital is about creating an ecosystem where sustainability and employee well-being coexist harmoniously. This symbiosis is the cornerstone of a thriving, future-forward organization.

Training and Education for the Green Economy

As we move forward in our journey towards sustainable transformation, it's crucial to recognise the central role that training and education play in preparing our workforce for the green economy. Developing a well-equipped and knowledgeable team is not just a nice-to-have; it's imperative for the transition to a sustainable landscape.

The shift to a green economy demands a fundamental change in how businesses operate. This transformation affects all aspects of human capital, from acquiring new skills to adapting to innovative responsibilities. Mid-career professionals, in particular, stand at a unique vantage point. With years of experience under their belts, they are well-positioned to pivot towards sustainability-driven roles, given the right training and educational opportunities.

One cannot underestimate the importance of continuous learning in this context. The traditional job market is undergoing an overhaul, with new green jobs emerging while older positions become obsolete. Thus, adaptive learning is not merely beneficial; it's essential. Mid-career professionals must thus be agile, willing to embrace emerging technologies and methodologies that align with sustainability principles.

Incorporating sustainability into existing curricula across educational institutions and corporate training modules is a logical step. However, it goes beyond simply adding a few courses here and there. It involves redesigning entire educational frameworks to reflect the intricate interplay between business practices and environmental stewardship. Hence, this calls for partnerships between academia, industry, and governments to ensure a cohesive and comprehensive approach.

A robust training programme must include core subjects such as climate science, environmental regulations, sustainable supply chains, and renewable energy technologies. Yet, it must also delve into softer skills like change management, creative problem solving, and ethical decision-making. These are not just buzzwords; they are the cornerstones of effective leadership in a green economy.

To inspire action, you need a compelling narrative. Stories of industry leaders who have successfully integrated green practices into their operations can serve as powerful motivators. These case studies not only provide insights but also serve as a roadmap for others to follow. The objective is to show that the green economy is not an abstract concept; it's a tangible pathway that leads to both profitability and sustainability.

There's also a significant role for vocational training tailored specifically to the requirements of green jobs. There's a need for skilled technicians, engineers, and operators who are proficient in new technologies such as solar energy systems, electric vehicles, and sustainable agriculture. These vocational courses should be designed to provide hands-on experience and direct applicability.

Another vital aspect is the necessity of leadership development geared towards sustainability. Leaders must act as catalysts for change within their organisations. Equipping them with the knowledge and strategies to drive sustainability initiatives can make a world of difference. Leadership programmes should thus focus on inculcating a deep understanding of sustainable business models alongside the traditional management training.

Moreover, technology can play a pivotal role in facilitating this educational evolution. Online platforms, webinars, and virtual workshops provide flexibility and accessibility, making it easier for mid-career professionals to engage in learning without disrupting their current roles. E-learning modules focused on sustainability topics can be a game-changer, offering tailored content that can be accessed anytime, anywhere.

The role of mentorship cannot be overlooked either. Experienced professionals who have navigated the transition to green sectors can offer invaluable guidance to those looking to follow suit. Mentorship programmes can help bridge the gap between theoretical knowledge and practical application, fostering a culture of continuous improvement and lifelong learning.

Incentivising education and training efforts through policy measures is another avenue worth exploring. Tax breaks, grants, and other financial incentives can encourage businesses and individuals alike to invest in upskilling and reskilling. These policies can serve as accelerators, hastening the pace at which the workforce adapts to green economy requirements.

Internally, organisations should consider establishing sustainability committees or task forces responsible for championing green initiatives. Such groups can ensure that the company remains aligned with its sustainability goals while promoting a culture of constant learning and improvement. These committees can act as internal think tanks, generating innovative ideas and strategies for sustainable growth.

Ultimately, the responsibility of fostering a capable workforce doesn't lie solely with educational institutions or governments; it must be a collaborative effort. Businesses must take proactive steps to identify skill gaps and provide the necessary training to bridge these gaps. This collaborative approach ensures that the workforce is not just prepared but is enthusiastic and dedicated to contributing to a sustainable future.

The journey towards a green economy is undoubtedly challenging. Still, it brings forth the promise of a more resilient, equitable, and prosperous world. By investing in training and education, we are investing in people – their potential, their futures, and the collective well-being of our planet. This is not merely an investment in skills but an investment in our shared humanity.

Chapter 12:
Community Investment and Social Impact

Community investment and social impact are not just fashionable buzzwords; they're crucial pillars in the architecture of sustainable transformation. When businesses engage with communities, they create a symbiotic relationship that benefits both society and the company itself. This is more than philanthropy; it's about embedding long-term value creation in every facet of the organisation's operations.

Corporate Social Responsibility (CSR) serves as the cornerstone of community investment. However, modern CSR goes beyond donations and charitable events. Today, it's about creating systemic change, addressing societal issues, and fostering inclusive growth. Companies that excel in CSR don't merely respond to community needs; they anticipate them, turning potential challenges into opportunities. A commitment to social equity can be the catalyst that triggers wider economic and environmental benefits.

There are myriad examples of companies that have mastered the art of community investment. One noteworthy example is a global retailer that invested in local entrepreneurship in underserved regions. By providing resources, training, and financial backing, the company not only transformed local economies but also created a new customer base and improved its brand reputation. Similarly, a tech giant's initiative to bridge the digital divide in rural areas led to enhanced education and employment prospects, subsequently cultivating a new generation of tech-savvy citizens.

The broader impact of community investment is often profound and multi-dimensional. When communities thrive, businesses flourish. Healthier, more educated communities can offer a more skilled workforce, while improved living standards can reduce societal tensions and foster a more stable market environment. Importantly, these efforts don't just generate immediate returns; they build resilience and adaptability, valuable traits for any organisation facing the uncertainties of the future.

Ultimately, the true measure of a company's impact lies in its ability to contribute to the common good. By integrating community investment into the core of business strategy, organisations can unlock untold potential, both within and around them. This is a transformational journey that invites both personal and collective growth, one that promises to redefine the contours of success in the modern world.

Corporate Social Responsibility (CSR)

Corporate Social Responsibility, or CSR, transcends mere philanthropic gestures and exists at the very core of integrating ethical practices into business operations. For mid-career professionals keen to inspire sustainable transformation, understanding CSR is pivotal. It's not just a trend or a checkmark on a company's list of priorities. It's a strategic approach that drives long-term value for both businesses and the community.

The concept of CSR encompasses a broad spectrum of practices aimed at fostering a sustainable and socially responsible business environment. It includes everything from environmental stewardship to ethical labour practices and community engagement. As professionals, the challenge lies in weaving these principles into the very fabric of corporate strategy, ensuring they shift from peripheral considerations to central tenets of business operations.

At its best, CSR is a marriage between profit and purpose. Companies that master this balance often find themselves not only thriving but also leading their industries in innovation and customer loyalty. This isn't just theory; there's ample evidence that businesses committed to CSR tend to outperform their peers financially. They attract dedicated employees, foster innovation, and develop stronger customer bases.

Why does CSR matter so much in today's world? Because consumers are more informed and more demanding. Gone are the days when a company's sole responsibility was to its shareholders. The modern consumer demands transparency, authenticity, and ethical conduct. Companies that overlook CSR risk alienating their customer base and falling behind in an increasingly competitive market.

But what does effective CSR look like? It begins with leadership. Leaders must embed sustainable practices and ethical considerations into their decision-making processes. This isn't about surface-level changes or public relations stunts. It's about real, tangible commitment. When leaders prioritise CSR, it cascades down throughout the organisation, influencing corporate culture and employee behaviours.

Moreover, CSR requires a strategic vision that aligns with the company's goals and values. This alignment ensures that CSR initiatives aren't just one-off projects but integral components of the business strategy. By setting clear objectives and measuring progress, companies can demonstrate their commitment to sustainable practices and showcase their impact.

Indispensable to successful CSR is transparent reporting. Using established frameworks, companies can measure and report on their

CSR initiatives, showcasing their achievements and areas for improvement. This transparency builds trust with stakeholders, from employees to customers and investors. When stakeholders see a company's genuine commitment to CSR, it strengthens relationships and fosters loyalty.

The community, an often-overlooked stakeholder, stands to benefit immensely from robust CSR practices. Companies that invest in social initiatives—be it education programmes, healthcare, or environmental projects—contribute to the social fabric and drive sustainable development. These initiatives can transform communities, boosting economic growth and improving quality of life.

In the realm of CSR, partnerships and collaborations amplify impact. By working with non-profits, government agencies, and other businesses, companies can leverage resources and expertise to tackle societal challenges. These collaborative efforts often yield more significant and lasting results, propelling both community enhancement and corporate success.

But CSR isn't without its challenges. Implementing these initiatives requires careful planning, resources, and a genuine commitment to long-term goals. It demands adaptability and resilience from organisations, especially when faced with resistance or economic pressures. Yet, the rewards—both tangible and intangible—are abundant.

Think about the broader impact of CSR: fostering a sustainable future for generations to come. When businesses operate responsibly, they not only benefit themselves but also contribute to the well-being of the planet and its people. This creates a cycle of prosperity—where sustainable business practices lead to healthier environments and societies, which in turn create more stable and prosperous markets.

CSR also brings about a shift in corporate mindset. It encourages businesses to think beyond short-term gains and focus on creating enduring value. This sustainable approach requires patience, dedication, and a willingness to innovate continually. But it is precisely this mindset that will drive the next wave of business success.

To be truly effective, CSR must be more than a set of policies—it has to become part of the company's DNA. This cultural shift ensures that every decision, big or small, is made with consideration for ethical, social, and environmental impact. When CSR is ingrained in the corporate ethos, it guides behaviour and decisions naturally.

Ultimately, CSR represents a transformative journey for businesses. It's a path that requires vision, commitment, and action. Yet for those willing to undertake this journey, the rewards are multifaceted—ranging from enhanced reputation and strengthened stakeholder relationships to tangible business growth and societal benefits.

As mid-career professionals, we have the power to champion CSR within our circles of influence. By advocating for and implementing responsible practices, we not only drive change but also set the stage for the sustainable transformation our world so desperately needs.

Case Studies of Community Investment

Consider the thriving urban centre of Phoenix, Arizona. Once blighted by economic downturns and plagued by social disconnect, it's a city that's transformed through strategic community investment. Take the example of the local housing redevelopment initiative led by the non-profit organisation FutureBuild. By securing public-private partnerships, they raised millions to revitalise disused properties into affordable housing units.

FutureBuild's success lay in their inclusive approach. They didn't just build houses; they fostered a sense of community. From the outset, they engaged local residents in the planning process, creating spaces that reflected the needs and desires of those who would live there. They didn't stop at physical infrastructure. They integrated job training programs, creating new employment opportunities for residents, and collaborated with local businesses to provide essential services.

Community investment doesn't start and end with brick and mortar. Consider the social enterprise GrowGreen in London. Facing food deserts in low-income neighbourhoods, GrowGreen didn't just open grocery stores; they transformed the community's approach to food. Through urban farming initiatives, local people were trained to grow their own produce using sustainable methods. It became a movement of empowerment, bridging gaps between socio-economic divides, reinforcing a sense of ownership and pride in the community.

In Cincinnati, Ohio, the civic project Community Health Forward serves as another beacon of successful community investment. Recognising the correlation between health and social equity, the initiative focused on healthcare accessibility in underserved areas. By investing in mobile clinics and digital health platforms, they bridged the healthcare gap. Their holistic approach didn't just treat symptoms but tackled root causes by offering educational programs on nutrition, mental health services, and preventative care practices.

Similarly, the Detroit Revitalisation Project offers insights into community investment's transformative power. It started with the humble goal of renovating abandoned storefronts. However, by involving artists, entrepreneurs, and community leaders, the project evolved into a cultural renaissance. Art galleries, artisan shops, and startup incubators now populate once-desolate neighbourhoods, breathing life and economic activity back into the city.

A case study from the rural town of Garforth in England illustrates how community energy projects can foster sustainability and economic growth. Garforth Power, a community-owned energy initiative, installed solar panels and wind turbines, reducing the town's carbon footprint and energy costs. Profits from the energy production were channelled back into the community, funding local schools, park renovations, and social services.

Take a look at Curitiba in Brazil, often celebrated as one of the greenest cities in the world. This didn't happen overnight. Investments in public transport, green spaces, and waste management from the 1970s transformed it. Perhaps the most remarkable aspect of Curitiba's success is the integrated approach to sustainability, where environmental policies supported economic and social welfare. The city invested in comprehensive recycling programs, coupled with educational campaigns, turning environmental stewardship into a community endeavour.

The small town of Totnes in Devon, England, offers a fascinating example through its local currency, the Totnes Pound. Designed to support independent businesses and strengthen the local economy, the currency kept money circulating within the community. By investing in a localised economic system, Totnes fostered economic resilience and bolstered community spirit.

In a different vein, the digital platform Kiva allows individuals to invest in communities globally through microloans. Kiva's model connects people willing to lend as little as $25 with small business owners and entrepreneurs in need. This direct approach to community investment has led to substantial economic development in impoverished regions, enabling beneficiaries to lift themselves out of poverty while investors witness the tangible impact of their contributions.

Looking at the educational sector, the Harlem Children's Zone in New York provides a comprehensive case study. By investing in education as a cornerstone of community development, the initiative offers a pipeline of support services from birth through college. From early childhood programs to charter schools and health clinics, the project embodies a holistic investment in the community's future, demonstrating that educational attainment is inextricably linked to economic and social wellbeing.

The San Francisco Bay Area's Tech Equity Collaborative represents how the technology sector can contribute to community investment. Focused on addressing the socio-economic impacts of the tech boom, the initiative works on affordable housing, job training, and policy advocacy. They engage tech companies directly, urging them to understand their role in local economies and incentivising them to invest back into the community.

Across the Atlantic, Berlin's cooperative housing model showcases another successful community investment strategy. Residents collectively own the housing projects, making decisions democratically. This model has stabilized housing costs and strengthened communal bonds by providing affordable living spaces and fostering a sense of shared responsibility.

On a broader scale, the Grameen Bank in Bangladesh showcases community investment's power in transforming economies. By providing microcredit to the rural poor, primarily women, the bank enabled recipients to start small businesses, thus fostering micro-enterprise. The ripple effects were profound, impacting social structures, improving education and healthcare access, and reducing poverty rates dramatically.

Micro-hydro projects in Nepal present a niche example of how community investment can bring sustainable energy to remote areas. By harnessing local waterways, these small-scale energy projects provide electricity, support local economies, and reduce dependence on non-renewable energy sources. Communities are directly involved in maintaining these projects, ensuring long-term sustainability and ownership.

Yet, perhaps the most poignant case study lies in Rwanda's National Unity and Reconciliation Commission. Following the 1994 genocide, the Rwandan government invested heavily in reconciling communities. Through initiatives like community courts (Gacaca) and local dialogues, they rebuilt social cohesion. The investment wasn't merely financial but deeply emotional and cultural, healing a fractured nation and paving the way for lasting peace and development.

These case studies illustrate that when done right, community investment is a powerful catalyst for sustainable transformation. Each example underscores a fundamental truth: transformative change doesn't come from isolated efforts but from integrated, inclusive approaches. Investing in communities is about creating environments where individuals feel empowered, valued, and connected. It's a mosaic of small and large actions collectively driving towards a brighter, more sustainable future.

Chapter 13:
Global Trends and Future Outlook

As we navigate the inexhaustible landscape of global finance and sustainable transformation, it's crucial to examine the evolving trends knitting our world closer together. The deck is being reshuffled, with emerging markets at the forefront, as they break away from traditional economic paradigms. Countries like China and India aren't just catching up—they're defining new standards in sustainability, as they robustly invest in green technologies and renewable energies. This shift offers a dual advantage: meeting their burgeoning domestic needs while positioning themselves as leaders in eco-economic capabilities.

Globally, the enduring focus on sustainability has given rise to a movement that's not just localised but intrinsically collaborative. As government policies align and corporate strategies converge, an era of unprecedented collective action is dawning. Financial markets are beginning to reflect these changes, with sustainable investments no longer being a niche. With ESG metrics becoming core to valuation, the future teems with opportunities for mid-career professionals, business leaders, and investors who can adeptly navigate these waters. The potential for growth and innovation has never been more substantial or more urgent.

Predicting the future is inherently fraught with uncertainty, but some trends are clear. Climate change mitigation will continue to dominate agendas, driving innovations in everything from smart grids to sustainable agriculture. Advancements in artificial intelligence and data analytics provide tools that can unearth inefficiencies and optimise processes on an unprecedented scale. Collaboration across sectors and borders will be indispensable, merging resources and expertise to craft durable, scalable solutions. The canvases of the future are blank, but the brushstrokes of today—the investments, policies, and innovations we deploy—will colour tomorrow's narrative.

Emerging Markets and Global Movement

The landscape of sustainability is evolving rapidly, and nowhere is this more apparent than in emerging markets. These regions, traditionally seen as the new frontier for economic growth, are now stepping into the spotlight for their potential to lead sustainable transformation. The global movement isn't just confined to the advanced economies; it is a worldwide awakening. Emerging markets are seizing the moment, reshaping their future, and in the process, redefining the global narrative around sustainability.

Emerging markets possess a unique advantage. They are not burdened by legacy infrastructures that dominate the industrialised world. This absence of entrenched systems allows them to leapfrog directly to greener technologies and sustainable practices. In many ways, they have the potential to become the crucibles of innovation, testing grounds for new ideas, and models of sustainable development.

Consider the rapid urbanisation happening in regions like Africa, Southeast Asia, and Latin America. This urbanisation presents both challenges and opportunities. On one hand, the demand for resources and energy is accelerating. On the other hand, there is an unparalleled opportunity to build smart, eco-friendly cities from the ground up. It's an opportunity to reimagine urban living with a green core, integrating renewable energy, sustainable transport, and efficient waste management systems.

Moreover, the demographic composition of these markets is another crucial factor. With a young, dynamic population, there's an inherent adaptability and openness to change. The youth aren't just passive recipients of this change; they are active participants, driving innovation and advocating for more sustainable, mindful consumption patterns. Their impatience with the status quo is a powerful catalyst for change.

Financial flows are also shifting towards these burgeoning regions. Investment in green technologies and sustainable projects in emerging markets has seen a marked increase. This influx of capital is a testament to the growing confidence in the potential of these markets. It's not philanthropy driving this investment, but an understanding that sustainability and profitability are not mutually exclusive.

In tandem with investments, international collaborations are flourishing. Governments, NGOs, and private enterprises from advanced economies are forming partnerships with stakeholders in emerging markets. These collaborations are grounded in a shared vision of a sustainable future and a mutual benefit. Knowledge transfer, technology sharing, and co-development of projects are becoming the norm rather than the exception.

Let's not overlook the importance of policy frameworks conducive to sustainable growth. Countries like India, Brazil, and South Africa are implementing robust policies aimed at encouraging renewable energy and sustainable practices. These policies are often ambitious, setting targets that push the envelope on what's achievable. It's this audacity in policy-making that propels substantive on-ground change.

Looking at the cultural dimensions, sustainability is deeply resonant with many traditional practices in emerging markets. For example, the concept of "ubuntu" in Africa, which emphasises community interconnectedness, aligns naturally with sustainable principles. Similarly, indigenous practices in many Latin American and

Asian communities have long cherished environmental stewardship. Such cultural synergies provide a fertile ground for embedding sustainability at the grassroots level.

The digital revolution also plays a critical role. Mobile technology and the internet are driving unprecedented access to information and services. In rural and remote areas, where traditional infrastructure development may lag, digital solutions are filling the gaps. This digital inclusion supports better education on sustainable practices, financial inclusivity for green investments, and new business models that align profit with purpose.

One can't discuss emerging markets without acknowledging the role of micro, small, and medium enterprises (MSMEs). They form the backbone of these economies and are crucial for social and economic stability. Empowering these enterprises with the tools and resources to adopt sustainable practices not only enhances their competitiveness but also ushers in widespread, inclusive sustainability.

The ripple effect of these efforts is global. As emerging markets embrace sustainable transformation, they influence global supply chains, pushing multinational corporations to adopt greener practices. This symbiotic relationship highlights that sustainable transformation is not a series of isolated events but a cohesive global movement.

There's also an ethical imperative at play. For advanced economies that have historically driven global emissions, supporting sustainable development in emerging markets is not just a strategic choice but a moral responsibility. The disparities in carbon footprints underscore the necessity for a balanced approach, where the global north aids the global south in achieving sustainable parity.

Yet, challenges persist. Infrastructure gaps, policy inconsistencies, and socio-economic inequalities must be navigated deftly. However, the resilience and ingenuity innate to these regions often find ways to turn obstacles into opportunities. This resilience, coupled with a strong sense of community, makes emerging markets fertile ground for sustainable transformation.

No discussion would be complete without addressing the concept of future-proofing. Emerging markets are acutely aware of the risks posed by climate change. This awareness drives a pragmatic approach to building systems and practices that not only address present needs but also safeguard against future uncertainties.

The shift in emerging markets towards sustainability is not just a regional phenomenon; it is a beacon of what's possible when there is a collective will for change. It's a call to action for the rest of the world, proving that sustainable transformation is within reach, not through grandiose, top-down mandates, but through community-led, innovation-driven, and inclusive practices.

Predicting Future Trends

In navigating the complex tapestry of tomorrow's world, predicting future trends in sustainability demands a nuanced understanding of the present. We stand at a crossroads where the decisions made today will significantly influence the trajectory of global markets, societal norms, and environmental health. Laying the groundwork for a sustainable future requires more than foresight; it requires action rooted in deep awareness and commitment to innovation.

One of the most compelling forecasts centres around the accelerated adoption of green technologies. The convergence of digital and sustainable advances promises to redefine industries from agriculture to automotive. Companies that can harness the power of artificial intelligence and machine learning for sustainability will find themselves at the forefront of this transformation. These technologies not only enhance operational efficiencies but also provide critical data insights, enabling smarter, more sustainable choices.

Another notable trend is the increasing influence of consumers who prioritise sustainability. As awareness grows, consumers are becoming more discerning and demanding transparency and ethical practices. Brands that fail to adapt will face reputational risks and dwindling market share. On the other hand, businesses that authentically embed sustainability into their core values and operations will cultivate loyalty and trust, key drivers for long-term success.

Regulatory landscapes are also evolving at a rapid pace. Governments worldwide are imposing stricter environmental regulations and incentivising sustainable practices. Compliance isn't just a legal obligation; it's a competitive advantage. Forward-thinking companies are not waiting for mandates but are voluntarily exceeding regulatory expectations, setting new standards within their industries.

Investment trends are shifting towards sustainability as well. Environmental, Social, and Governance (ESG) criteria are becoming critical in investment decisions. Investors are increasingly scrutinising companies' sustainability records, driving capital towards those with robust ESG frameworks. This trend reflects a broader understanding that sustainable investments often yield long-term benefits, both financially and socially.

Materials science is another field undergoing significant transformation. Innovations in biodegradable materials and sustainable resource utilisation are paving the way for a circular economy. This shift aims to minimise waste and maximise the lifecycle of products, disrupting traditional linear economies. Companies that spearhead these innovations will not only contribute to environmental preservation but also create new economic opportunities.

The future labour market will also experience substantial changes. Jobs centred around sustainability will become more prevalent. This shift necessitates a rethinking of education and training programs to equip the workforce with necessary skills. Companies investing in the development of their human capital will not only foster a knowledgeable workforce but also drive innovation and sustainability from within.

Urbanisation trends indicate that smart cities will become the norm rather than the exception. Integrating sustainable infrastructure with digital technology will create environments that are not only livable but also reduce resource consumption. Surveillance, electric mobility, and renewable energy systems will collectively transform urban living, making cities more resilient and sustainable.

Global geopolitical dynamics will play a crucial role in shaping the sustainability landscape. Collaboration between countries on climate policies and sustainable practices will determine the pace of global transformation. Multilateral agreements and partnerships will be essential in addressing global challenges that transcend national borders, such as climate change and biodiversity loss.

Corporate responsibility will continue to expand beyond mere profitability to include social and environmental stewardship. Companies will need to embrace a broader definition of success, one that incorporates their impact on the planet and society. As stakeholder capitalism gains traction, businesses will be measured against their contributions to societal well-being.

Technological democratisation will also drive change. With advancements making technology more accessible, smaller enterprises and startups will have the opportunity to innovate and compete on a larger scale. These newcomers can be nimbler and more adaptable, often leading the way in sustainable practices and solutions.

One cannot ignore the significance of social movements in shaping the future. The voices advocating for climate justice, equality, and ethical consumption are becoming louder and more influential. These societal shifts will pressurise companies and governments to act responsibly and equitably, further accelerating the pace of sustainable transformation.

R&D for sustainable solutions will be pivotal. Investing in research and development focused on sustainability will not only drive innovation but also uncover new opportunities and markets. Companies that prioritise R&D in sustainability are likely to discover groundbreaking solutions that can provide them with a competitive edge.

Consumer behaviour analytics will become a key tool in predicting and shaping future trends. By understanding and anticipating consumer preferences, businesses can align their strategies to meet the growing demand for sustainable products and services. Utilising data-driven insights will be essential in staying ahead of the curve.

The intersection of finance and sustainability will reimagine traditional economic models. Concepts like green bonds and carbon credits will become integral to financial planning and operations. As these financial instruments mature, they'll provide more options for companies and investors to fund and prioritise sustainable initiatives.

In summary, predicting future trends in sustainability isn't an exercise in speculation; it's a call to action. The momentum towards a sustainable future is undeniable and accelerating. Professionals who align with these trends and adapt proactively will not only enhance their competitiveness but also contribute significantly to the broader goal of building a sustainable world. The future belongs to those who anticipate change and act with foresight and purpose.

Chapter 14:
Overcoming Barriers to Sustainable Transformation

As we dig deeper into the journey towards sustainable transformation, it's important to address the barriers that often stand in the way. Many organisations find themselves staring at seemingly insurmountable obstacles, but these barriers are not walls; they are hurdles that can be overcome with the right approach and mindset.

One of the most persistent challenges is the perception that sustainability is an additional cost rather than an investment. This narrow view overlooks the long-term benefits and savings. Organisations that embrace eco-friendly practices often witness reduced operational costs, enhanced brand loyalty, and a stronger marketplace position. To shift this mindset, it's essential to present data-driven evidence and case studies that demonstrate successful transformations, showing that sustainability can indeed drive profitability.

Another significant barrier is the inertia of existing corporate culture. Changing deep-rooted habits and mindsets isn't easy, but it's imperative. Successful transformational stories often start with a clear vision from leadership. When leaders commit to sustainable goals and integrate them into the company's core values, they pave the way for a cultural shift. Moreover, fostering an environment that encourages innovation and open communication can dismantle resistance and fuel a collective effort towards sustainability.

Common Challenges and Solutions

In the journey towards sustainable transformation, mid-career professionals often encounter a myriad of challenges. These obstacles can sometimes seem insurmountable, deterring even the most steadfast advocates. However, understanding these common challenges and the strategic solutions to overcome them can turn impediments into stepping stones.

1. Resistance to Change: One of the primary hurdles is resistance to change. People are creatures of habit, and altering long-standing practices disrupts comfort zones. Encouraging change requires not just demonstrating the necessity but also highlighting the benefits. Leaders must cultivate a culture that embraces change through transparent communication and inclusive decision-making processes.

2. Lack of Awareness: Many professionals are unfamiliar with the underlying principles and advantages of sustainable practices. To counteract this, continuous education and training programmes can be instituted. Companies should invest in learning resources that help employees understand how sustainability is not just ethical but also financially beneficial.

3. Financial Constraints: Another significant barrier is the perceived high cost of implementing sustainable practices. However, by approaching sustainability as a long-term investment rather than a short-term expenditure, businesses can reap substantial financial rewards. Exploring various financing options, such as green bonds or sustainability-linked loans, can make the initial outlay more manageable.

4. Complexity in Measurement: Measuring the impact of sustainable initiatives can be daunting. The lack of standardised metrics often leads to inconsistent reporting. Introducing robust KPIs and adhering to recognised reporting frameworks can bring clarity and comparability. Leveraging technology to track and analyse data can also simplify the process.

5. Short-Term Focus: The pressure to deliver quick financial returns often overshadows long-term sustainability goals. Cultivating a shift in mindset within the organisation from short-termism to long-term value creation is essential. This requires strong leadership and a commitment to integrating sustainability into the core strategy of the business.

6. Insufficient Policy Support: Government regulations play a crucial role in facilitating sustainable transformation. However, inconsistent or inadequate policy support can hinder progress. Active engagement with policymakers to advocate for supportive legislation and incentives can create a more favourable environment for sustainable practices.

7. Technological Limitations: Many companies struggle with outdated technology that is not conducive to sustainable operations. Investing in green technology and fostering innovation within the organisation can bridge this gap. Collaborating with tech companies and researchers can also provide access to cutting-edge solutions.

8. Cultural Barriers: In multinational corporations, varying cultural perspectives on sustainability can pose challenges. Promoting a unified vision and establishing global sustainability standards can help mitigate these differences. Encouraging cross-cultural exchanges and understanding can foster a more cohesive approach.

9. Supply Chain Issues: Ensuring sustainability throughout the supply chain can be complex. From sourcing raw materials to manufacturing processes, every link in the chain must align with sustainable practices. Developing strong relationships with suppliers and integrating sustainability criteria into the procurement process are vital steps.

10. Ineffective Communication: Even with the best intentions, ineffective communication can derail sustainable initiatives. Clear, consistent, and engaging communication strategies are necessary to keep all stakeholders informed and motivated. Utilising various platforms to share progress and success stories can build momentum and support.

11. Leadership Gaps: Leadership can make or break sustainability efforts. Leaders must be visibly committed to sustainable transformation, setting the tone from the top. Offering leadership development programmes focused on sustainability can equip leaders with the necessary skills and knowledge to drive change.

12. Stakeholder Alignment: Aligning diverse stakeholder groups around common sustainability goals can be challenging. Regular dialogue, transparency, and demonstrated benefits can build trust and buy-in. Constructing a stakeholder engagement plan that addresses concerns and aligns interests is crucial.

13. Balancing Trade-offs: Sustainable transformation often involves making trade-offs between various economic, environmental, and social factors. An honest assessment of these trade-offs and a balanced approach that considers long-term impacts are essential. Scenario planning can help identify and mitigate potential conflicts.

14. Overcoming Cynicism: Skepticism about the efficacy of sustainable practices can undermine efforts. Showcasing evidence-based success stories and demonstrating tangible benefits can dispel doubts and build confidence. Openness to feedback and continuous improvement can also reinforce credibility.

15. Integrating with Existing Operations: Incorporating sustainability into existing operations without disrupting business can be tricky. A phased approach that gradually integrates sustainable practices can ease the transition. Pilot projects can serve as testing grounds before a full-scale roll-out.

The path to sustainable transformation is fraught with obstacles, but these barriers are not insurmountable. By understanding and addressing these common challenges, mid-career professionals can pave the way for meaningful and lasting change. The key lies in resilience, adaptability, and a steadfast commitment to a sustainable future.

Stories of Overcoming Obstacles

Every great journey towards sustainable transformation is littered with significant obstacles. These hurdles, while often daunting, serve as the crucibles in which resilience, innovation, and true commitment are forged. Let's delve into real-world stories that elucidate how some have navigated these challenges and emerged on the other side, stronger and more capable.

Imagine a manufacturing firm confined by decades-old practices that leaned heavily on fossil fuels. The top brass knew that sustainability was no longer an option but a necessity. However, transitioning to greener energy wasn't merely flipping a switch; it was about overhauling an entire system deeply entrenched in its ways.

Faced with significant resistance from various departments concerned about costs and disruptions, the company's leadership initiated a pilot project. They selected one small plant for a renewable energy makeover, installing solar panels and implementing energy-efficient machinery. Initial results were promising: operational costs dropped, and the unit's carbon footprint significantly reduced.

Buoyed by this success, the company expanded the initiative to more facilities. While initial investments were substantial, the firm experienced long-term savings and gained a competitive edge. By confronting resistance with data-backed success, they gradually won over skeptics, transforming resistance into commitment.

Tech industries often face unique obstacles due to their rapid pace of innovation and fierce competition. A burgeoning start-up aimed to be at the forefront of sustainable tech, developing devices that consumed less power. However, as they scaled, production costs soared, and delivering on sustainability became increasingly challenging.

Their breakthrough came when they forged a partnership with a supplier equally committed to sustainability. This collaboration not only reduced costs through shared research and development but also set a new standard in the industry. The lesson was clear: sustainable success often relies on forging the right alliances.

One cannot ignore the complexities that multinational corporations encounter. Operating across borders introduces a host of variables—different regulatory landscapes, divergent market expectations, and diverse cultural attitudes toward sustainability. For one global conglomerate, achieving uniform sustainability practices seemed an insurmountable task.

They tackled this challenge by establishing regional sustainability hubs. Each hub was empowered to adapt central sustainability goals to local circumstances, ensuring relevance and feasibility. Moreover, they held annual global sustainability summits, where regional leaders shared insights and strategies. This local-global synergy made what seemed impossible, achievable.

Consider the agricultural sector, notorious for its deep-rooted, traditional practices. A family-owned farm, operational for generations, aimed to transition to organic farming. The obstacles were manifold—higher costs, steep learning curves, and market unpredictability.

The farm adopted a phased approach, converting small sections to organic practices and observing outcomes. They also engaged in community-supported agriculture (CSA), which allowed them to build a local customer base that valued organic produce. These loyal customers provided the financial buffer required to expand sustainable practices across the entire farm. Their story is a testament to the power of gradual, community-backed transformation.

Another intriguing story hails from the fashion industry, infamous for its environmental impact. A mid-sized clothing company sought to revolutionize how clothing was produced and disposed of. Understanding that pure innovation wasn't enough, they embarked on a transparent journey, documenting each step and setback on social media.

This transparency fostered a strong brand identity and gained them a loyal customer base more interested in supporting genuine efforts over mere greenwashing. They turned every obstacle into a learning opportunity, freely sharing their findings with the broader industry, sparking widespread change.

Let's not overlook the public sector, often perceived as slow-moving and bureaucratic. Nevertheless, an urban planning department in a bustling city proved that even public institutions could not only adopt but champion sustainability. Initially overwhelmed by antiquated infrastructure and limited budgets, they decided to leverage technology and community engagement to drive change.

They introduced smart city technologies that improved energy efficiency and waste management. More importantly, they involved residents in the decision-making process, making them stakeholders in the city's sustainable future. This collective effort yielded remarkable transformations in urban sustainability, setting a model for other cities to follow.

A health care provider faced the dual challenge of maintaining high-quality care while transitioning to sustainable practices. Initially, the complexities of medical waste management and energy consumption seemed insurmountable. However, by investing in green building technology and fostering a culture of sustainability among staff, they gradually made headway. Their persistent efforts resulted in a healthier environment for both patients and the planet.

In each of these stories, the common thread is persisting through adversity, pooling collective expertise, and maintaining unwavering commitment to sustainable goals. The convergence of these elements not only addresses obstacles head-on but transforms them into enablers of lasting change.

Success in sustainable transformation is not merely about reaching the destination but embracing the journey with all its hardships and triumphs. These stories serve as beacons, illuminating the path for those who dare to envision and work towards a sustainable future.

Let these narratives inform your journey, lighting the way through the seemingly insurmountable to reach a world where sustainability is the norm, not the exception.

Chapter 15:
Taking Action: Your Role in
Sustainable Transformation

As we've navigated the landscape of sustainable transformation, it's clear that the journey is as much about personal commitment as it is about strategic frameworks and corporate strategies. In the realm of business, we often look to data, metrics, and models to guide our decisions. But none of these tools will drive substantial change without the conscious choices and actions of individuals like you. This chapter is about embracing your role in this broader movement, reflecting on how your daily actions and professional decisions can cascade into a broader impact.

First, take a moment for personal reflection. Look around you - at your workspace, your projects, your team. Are there habits or practices that can be tweaked towards sustainability? Sometimes, it's as simple as making the switch to digital documents, reducing travel by opting for virtual meetings, or encouraging energy-saving practices in the office. While these changes may seem small, they create a ripple effect, influencing colleagues, company policies, and eventually, market trends. Change, after all, starts at the micro level.

Consider how you can integrate sustainable practices into your professional life. Are you in a position to influence procurement policies? Advocate for suppliers who follow ethical and sustainable practices. If investment decisions fall within your purview, push for more funds to be allocated to green technology and sustainable ventures. Even if you're not in a leadership role, you can still drive change by participating in or initiating sustainability committees and feedback loops within your organisation.

Practical steps for immediate action are within your grasp. Begin by setting clear and achievable goals, both short-term and long-term. Commit to continuous learning by attending workshops, webinars, and reading up on the latest sustainability trends and innovations. Use the tools and templates provided in Appendix A to draft action plans and measure progress. Collaborate with like-minded professionals and create a network of sustainability champions within your industry. This collective effort can accelerate the shift towards a more sustainable business environment.

Finally, remember that every small action contributes to the larger cause. Sustainable transformation is not just a corporate agenda; it's a personal commitment. Let this commitment guide your decisions, inform your strategies, and inspire those around you. Together, through concerted and conscious efforts, we can make meaningful strides towards a sustainable future, leaving a lasting legacy for generations to come.

Personal Reflection and Commitment

As we move through the intricate tapestry of sustainable transformation, it's crucial we pause and turn the lens inward. Self-reflection isn't just an exercise in mindfulness; it's the foundation upon which our commitment to sustainable action is built. Mid-career, you've seen the ebbs and flows of industry trends. You've gained insights that newcomers can't yet fathom. It's precisely this wealth of experience that positions you perfectly to drive change. But before you can inspire others, it's essential to align your actions with your convictions.

Think back to why you entered your profession in the first place. Was it the allure of financial stability, personal ambition, or perhaps a passion for making a difference? It's easy to lose sight of these motivations in the daily grind. However, recalling your initial inspiration can rekindle a sense of purpose that's crucial for long-term sustainable engagement. When you connect with that original fire, you find a well of energy that can sustain your efforts against the tide of inertia and resistance.

Consider the principles and ethics that have guided you thus far. They are your compass. Reflect on moments when choices aligned or diverged from these values. What were the outcomes? Sustainable transformation requires a resolute adherence to ethical standards, often in the face of short-term gains that tempt deviation. By personally committing to these values, you lay a robust foundation for collective action within your organisation and beyond.

It's time to scrutinise your professional habits and routines. In your day-to-day activities, where can you implement more sustainable practices? This isn't about grand gestures; it's about consistency. Maybe it's opting for digital reports over printed ones, or consistently pushing for suppliers with sustainable practices. Small, habitual changes compound over time, creating a profound impact. Moreover, as a mid-career professional, your actions are observed and often emulated by juniors. This ripple effect magnifies your personal commitment exponentially.

Let's talk about time—the scarcest resource. Reflect on how you allocate your time, both professionally and personally. How much of it is devoted to driving or supporting sustainable initiatives? Realign your priorities to reflect your commitment. Attend to sustainability-focused conferences, workshops, or even casual networking events that put you in touch with like-minded professionals. Enriching your knowledge and network can reveal new opportunities and collaborations that you hadn't considered.

In conclusion, think of how your journey can inspire others. Stories are powerful tools for change. Share your challenges, triumphs, and even failures with your peers and subordinates. Your transparency not only builds trust but also motivates others to take their own steps towards sustainable action. Remember, commitment isn't a one-time pledge; it's a continuous journey of reflection, action, and reassessment. Each step you take not only paves the way for your own sustainable transformation but also for those following in your footsteps.

So, where do you begin? Start with a quiet moment of introspection, acknowledging the complexities and contradictions of your current practices. Then, make a personal commitment to change. Whether it's shifting a small habit or advocating for larger systemic improvements, know that every action counts. Your role in sustainable transformation starts with a committed mind and heart—everything else naturally follows.

Practical Steps for Immediate Action

We stand on the shoulders of transformative ideals, ready to leap into action. As seasoned professionals with a firm grasp on finance and investing, you possess the expertise needed to bring sustainable principles into everyday practice. Here's how you can roll up your sleeves and get started straight away.

Firstly, reassess your current investments through the lens of sustainability. Scrutinise your portfolio and identify assets that align with eco-friendly values. Divest from sectors that exacerbate environmental degradation and reinvest in green alternatives. Transitioning capital may seem like a small step, but it undoubtedly marks the beginning of a significant shift.

Consider building a coalition within your company. Engage with like-minded colleagues and form a sustainability task force. This group's aim should be to brainstorm actionable initiatives, document achievable goals, and set timelines. A cohesive team can amplify individual efforts and bring about meaningful change within your organisation.

Next, champion energy efficiency within your office environment. From something as simple as switching to energy-efficient LED lighting, to more comprehensive measures like installing smart meters and monitoring energy use, every action counts. Promote policies that encourage remote working; even partial remote options can reduce a company's carbon footprint considerably.

Initiate or participate in waste reduction programmes. Begin with a comprehensive audit to understand where waste is coming from and how it can be minimised. Adopt practices like composting food waste, recycling office supplies, and using digital documentation to cut down on paper usage. Aim to foster a culture where waste reduction is second nature.

Don't shy away from influence. Leverage your role to advocate for sustainable procurement practices. Insist on choosing suppliers with green credentials and transparency when it comes to their sustainability efforts. Establishing long-term relationships with eco-conscious vendors can lead to mutually beneficial growth.

Incorporate sustainability into your company's training programmes. Equip your workforce with knowledge about eco-friendly practices and the importance of a sustainable future. When employees understand the 'why' and 'how' of sustainability, they become an integral part of the transformation journey.

Track progress meticulously. Utilise sustainable metrics and key performance indicators (KPIs) specially designed for your industry.

Data-driven insights will help you gauge the impact of your initiatives and make necessary adjustments. Regular reports can hold everyone accountable and celebrate small victories along the way.

Engage with the community. Corporate social responsibility initiatives can extend beyond the office. Partner with local green businesses, support environmental projects, and participate in community clean-ups. These efforts enhance your corporate image and build a more sustainable, unified local economy.

Finally, stay curious and continually educate yourself. The field of sustainability is evolving rapidly, and staying updated on emerging trends, new technologies, and policy changes is crucial. Attend industry conferences, read relevant publications, and participate in webinars to keep your knowledge fresh and actionable.

In these steps and beyond, there's no need to strive for perfection immediately. Aim for continuous improvement. Small, consistent changes can culminate in powerful transformations. Sustainable actions aren't just about the grand gestures; they thrive on everyday decisions that collectively map out a brighter, more resilient future.

Conclusion:
A Roadmap to a Sustainable Future

We stand at a critical juncture in history, where the choices we make today will define the world for generations to come. The journey of this book has taken you through the complex but rewarding landscape of sustainable transformation. From understanding the historical context and financial implications to integrating sustainability into corporate strategies, we've traversed a wide array of terrains. Now, as we reach the conclusion, it's time to chart a course forward, a roadmap to a sustainable future.

Every step along this journey underscores one irrefutable truth: sustainability isn't a mere buzzword; it's a necessity. Companies that embed sustainable practices within their DNA don't just survive—they thrive. We've seen how profitability and competitiveness can coalesce with ecological stewardship to create a robust and resilient business model. The narrative of eco-economics is a compelling one, but it demands actionable steps and consistent effort from all stakeholders—executives, employees, investors, and policymakers alike.

The financial realm has evolved to acknowledge the power and potential of sustainable investing. Key financial instruments like green bonds and sustainability-linked loans offer compelling avenues for channeling capital towards projects that make a real difference. By mastering these instruments, financial professionals can act as catalysts for positive change. But it's not just about leveraging the right tools;

it's also about fostering an investment culture that prioritises long-term ecological well-being over short-term gains.

Corporate strategy, too, needs to be reframed in the context of sustainability. Integration isn't a box-ticking exercise; it requires visionary leadership, robust governance, and an unwavering commitment to key performance indicators that capture true impact. Leadership has to emanate from the top but must permeate throughout the organisation. Only then can businesses cultivate an environment where innovation flourishes, risks are mitigated, and sustainable development becomes second nature.

Metrics and measurement frameworks, while often seen as tedious, are the backbone of any credible sustainability effort. By setting clear KPIs and adhering to recognised reporting standards, companies can not only track their progress but also communicate it effectively to stakeholders. In a world increasingly driven by transparency and accountability, these metrics serve as a foundation for trust, ensuring that sustainability claims are substantiated by real-world data.

Driving innovation remains a cornerstone of sustainable transformation. The pursuit of green technology and sustainable solutions requires a robust investment in research and development. It's an ongoing cycle of innovation, reflection, and improvement. By championing R&D efforts, companies can stay ahead of the curve, launching solutions that address not only today's challenges but also anticipate tomorrow's.

As risks around environmental sustainability escalate, effective risk management becomes indispensable. Identifying potential threats and devising strategies to mitigate them ensures resilience in the face of uncertainty. Building such resilience isn't an isolated task; it integrates into broader business operations, enhancing an organisation's ability to adapt and prosper in a fluctuating landscape.

Policy and regulation will always play a significant role in shaping sustainable practices. Engaging with policymakers while staying abreast of evolving regulations is crucial. These external forces, leveraged correctly, can serve as enablers of your sustainability agendas. Influencing policy from within the industry can drive systemic change, reflecting collective commitment to sustainability beyond mere compliance.

Perhaps the most profound takeaway from our exploration is the transformative power of collective action. While individual efforts are vital, it's the collective contributions of businesses, finance professionals, policymakers, and communities that will truly pave the way to a sustainable future. Steel yourselves with the knowledge and tools gained throughout this book, and act with conviction and purpose.

So, what lies on this roadmap to a sustainable future? It's a journey of continuous improvement, adaptability, and unyielding commitment. Each decision, no matter how small, reverberates through the ecosystem, contributing to a larger, collective impact. With strategic foresight and unwavering dedication, we can transcend the challenges ahead and foster a world where sustainable practices aren't the exception but the norm.

Appendix A:
Resources for Sustainable Business

As we come to the practical heart of our journey through sustainable transformation, this appendix offers a treasure trove of resources designed to bolster your strategies. You're already equipped with a conceptual understanding and now, it's time to delve into actionable tools that can concretely shape your day-to-day operations.

First off, let's talk about **auditing your current sustainability practices**. Platforms like *GRI Standards* and *SASB* offer extensive frameworks to measure your efforts accurately. These standards help you identify gaps and strengths in your approach and provide a structured pathway for improvement. For a broader scope, consider integrating the *United Nations' Sustainable Development Goals (SDGs)* into your strategy. They not only benchmark your progress but also align your business objectives with global missions.

Next, we turn to **software tools that aid in environmental impact assessments**. Tools like *Gaia* and *Simapro* are invaluable for Life Cycle Assessment (LCA), aiding in evaluating the environmental impact of products or services from cradle to grave. These platforms offer detailed analytical capabilities, enabling you to identify key areas where you can reduce environmental footprints effectively.

Investing in **green technology** stands as a pivotal step towards sustainability. Resources such as *Renewable Energy Buyers Alliance (REBA)* offer guidance on sourcing renewable energy and improving energy efficiency. These resources can help any business shift from reliance on fossil fuels to more sustainable energy options, a transformation that can bring profound competitive advantages.

When talking about raising capital for sustainable projects, look no further than platforms like *Green Bond Principles (GBP)* and *Sustainalytics*. These frameworks provide guidelines and assessment tools to ensure that your sustainability claims are robust, which can greatly enhance credibility with potential investors. Additionally, exploring ESG (Environmental, Social, and Governance) criteria through rating agencies like *MSCI* can make your business a more attractive candidate for socially responsible investment funds.

Another cornerstone is **education and training resources**. Institutes like the *Sustainability Accounting Standards Board (SASB) Institute* and the *Cambridge Institute for Sustainability Leadership* offer extensive training programs to help your workforce understand and embrace sustainability principles. Developing internal expertise is crucial for sustaining long-term transformation, ensuring that every department and team member aligns with overarching sustainability goals.

Supply chain sustainability can also be advanced with resources such as the *Carbon Disclosure Project (CDP)*. Suppliers are evaluated and screened based on their environmental practices, thereby ensuring that your supply chain maintains ethical and sustainable standards. Collaboration tools through *EcoVadis* further simplify the process of integrating sustainability throughout your procurement processes.

Communicating your sustainability efforts effectively is another challenge, readily addressed by tools like *Eco-Business* and *GreenBiz*. These platforms offer media services and frameworks for reporting your progress, helping you reach wider audiences and engage stakeholders compellingly.

For regulatory compliance, resources like the *European Union's Eco-Management and Audit Scheme (EMAS)* provide detailed guidelines and verification tools to ensure your practices meet stringent regulatory standards. Staying informed and compliant with these regulations is non-negotiable for maintaining the credibility and legality of your sustainability efforts.

Finally, tools and templates for **ongoing measurement and reporting** include frameworks like the *Integrated Reporting (IR) Framework* and *ISO 14001*. These guides help you draft thorough and comprehensible reports that reflect your sustainability journey's intricacies.

This appendix is your toolkit for actualising the theories and strategies discussed throughout this book. By leveraging these resources, you possess the capability to forge a path that transcends traditional business goals, reaching towards a sustainable future that's both profitable and ethical.

Tools and Templates for Implementation

Understanding the concepts and armed with the knowledge shared so far, it's time to delve into the practical side of sustainable transformation. In this section, we'll explore various tools and templates designed to assist you in implementing sustainability strategies within your organisation.

Sustainability isn't just a lofty ideal; it's a compilation of practical steps that need methodical planning and execution. Herein lies the importance of having well-crafted tools and templates at your disposal. They serve as guideposts, helping to navigate the complexities of incorporating sustainable practices into everyday business operations.

The right tools and templates not only streamline processes but also ensure consistency, transparency, and efficacy. Think of them as the scaffolding that supports the construction of a resilient, eco-conscious business model.

First, let's consider **assessment tools**. These are essential for evaluating your current sustainability status. Comprehensive assessment tools can help identify gaps, benchmark against industry standards, and set realistic targets. They might take the form of questionnaires, audit checklists, or software that tracks environmental impact.

Once you've gathered your preliminary data, you'll want templates to translate these findings into actionable plans. Here, *planning templates* become invaluable. They typically include sections for setting objectives, defining roles and responsibilities, and establishing timelines.

Next up are **tracking and reporting tools**. Continuous monitoring is vital for sustainable transformation. Spreadsheets and specialised software can track progress against pre-defined KPIs. Consistent reporting not only keeps your team aligned but also fosters accountability and transparency, which are crucial in engaging stakeholders and maintaining trust.

Let's not forget about **communication templates**. Effective communication strategies often hinge on clear, consistent messaging. Templates for internal updates, stakeholder reports, and press releases ensure that your sustainability efforts are communicated effectively. These templates can include predefined sections for key highlights, challenges, and future plans, making it easier to articulate your journey.

In addition to these fundamental tools, consider leveraging **collaborative platforms**. These can facilitate the exchange of ideas, foster innovation, and enhance team cohesion. Platforms like intranets or dedicated project management tools enable seamless collaboration and idea-sharing, fostering a culture of continuous improvement.

Moreover, templates for **training and development programs** are paramount. Training modules, workshop outlines, and skill assessment forms can accelerate capacity building within your team. Empowering your human capital with the necessary skills and knowledge is often the linchpin for a successful sustainable transformation.

Lastly, don't underestimate the power of **visual tools**. Diagrams, flowcharts, and infographics can simplify complex information and facilitate better understanding and retention. Whether it's charting your progress or mapping out new initiatives, visual tools can be exceptionally effective.

Embrace these tools and templates as extensions of your vision for a sustainable future. Remember, the journey of transformation calls for meticulous planning, consistent effort, and unwavering commitment. With the right tools at your disposal, you can navigate this journey with greater assurance and effectiveness, transforming aspirational goals into tangible outcomes.

www.ingramcontent.com/pod-product-compliance
Lightning Source LLC
Chambersburg PA
CBHW030524210326
41597CB00013B/1025